C.S. Lewis
AND HIS WORLD
David Barratt

Marshall Pickering/Wm. B. Eerdmans

Beginnings

An Ulster childhood

'... it is like nothing so much as the assembly of white foam caps when a fresh breeze is on a summer sea. And the roads are white too; there is no tarmac yet ... the whole country is a turbulent democracy of little hills ... not your hard English sunlight; make it paler, make it softer ... deepening it ... And beyond all this, so remote that they seem fantastically abrupt at the very limit of your vision, imagine the mountains.'

Such is the lyrical description Clive Staples Lewis gives to his birthplace, county Down in Northern Ireland. It comes from his autobiography *Surprised by Joy*, but it could have been from several of his letters, such was the abiding impression of Ulster on him. During his boyhood there, in the first years of the twentieth century, Northern Ireland did not exist as a political entity, as it does now, and so the region did not have the sad overtones of violence and division that it does for us

Below: 'Little Lea', the Lewises' family home from 1905. C.S. Lewis wrote: 'I am the product of long corridors, empty sunlit rooms, upstair indoor silences, attics explored in solitude...'

today. The term 'Ulster' meant for Lewis a beautiful area in a beautiful country, with a past that was more romantic than turbulent. Indeed, it has been suggested that if his invented land of Narnia is based on anything, it must be on the countryside of Ireland.

Lewis was born in 1898 in Belfast – not perhaps the most romantic of cities – but before he was very old, his parents had moved to what were then the outskirts, to a suburb called Strandtown. This was within walking and easy cycling distance of the countryside of county Down. Although he left home quite early to go to boarding school, and only returned for comparatively brief stays during his youth, C.S. Lewis remained closely in touch with the area all his life. Just before his death he was planning another of the summer holidays in Ireland that were his custom, especially with his boyhood friend, Arthur Greeves.

Although Lewis grew to love the English countryside too, his first impressions of England were very unfavourable. Writing from school in Malvern (which to many people is the epitome of England's beauty), he says to Arthur:

'It makes me furious to think of your being able to walk about your house and ours and all the beautiful places we know in the country while I am cooped up in this hot, ugly country of England...

'County Down must be looking glorious now ... The sunrise over the Holywood Hills, and the fresh stillness of the early morning are well worth the trouble of early rising...'

One of the features he clearly missed was the sea. 'I cannot bear to live too far away from it,' he writes. In fact he spent

The Lewis family. Standing: Lewis's father, Albert James Lewis, and his grandmother. Front row: Lewis's mother, Flora; his brother, Warren; his grandfather; his cousin, Irene; his Aunt Agnes; and Clive Staples Lewis.

most of his life well away from it, at Oxford; but Narnia is certainly full of the sea.

Although Ulster is not just a place, but a culture, and one that is often stigmatized as narrowly, even fanatically, religious, C.S. Lewis was never affected by this side of it. He tells Arthur Greeves in later life that he is neither attracted nor repelled by the 'Puritanism' he sees there. We may without doubt say that for Lewis, Ulster was a positive source of life and beauty, which was for him always universal and never provincial.

The Lewis family

The Lewises had only been Ulstermen for three generations – a relatively short time when compared with some of the Protestant families, such as the Hamiltons, his mother's side, who had settled there from Scotland in the reign of King James I and had at some stage become allied with even older, Anglo-Norman blood. His mother's family, then, touched on the Irish upper class; many

had become clergy, and one a bishop.

By contrast, the Lewises were working class people from the Wrexham area of North Wales. Grandfather Richard Lewis had emigrated to Ulster and done well in ship-building, showing considerable intelligence. His son Albert, Lewis's father, received a good education at Lurgan College, became a solicitor and married Florence Hamilton in 1894. She was a brilliant mathematician, having graduated from Queen's College, Belfast in 1885 with a first-class degree in logic and a second-class in mathematics. Their two sons were born in 1895 and 1898.

In *Surprised by Joy*, Lewis characterizes the two sides of the family emotionally: his father's Welsh side he sees as melancholic, very up-and-down and liable to unhappiness; whereas his mother's side was settled, happy and affectionate, critical and ironic. He certainly seems to have reacted against his father in a number of ways – Albert Lewis's intense absorption in politics left his son indifferent to them all his life; his father's overt emotionalism left C.S. Lewis afraid of outward displays of feelings. Always, too, he speaks of a fear of paternal abandonment, perhaps partly created by the early loss of his mother in August 1908, which also caused his father to retire into a personal grief, unable to carry his two sons through their loss.

Such circumstances made C.S. Lewis's relationship with his elder brother Warren ('Warnie', as he was always known, Lewis being known as 'Jack') very important to him. There was never any sibling rivalry between them. Throughout their life they co-operated closely together, and for a while, after his retirement from an army career, Warren acted as Jack's secretary and the family historian. The brothers' closeness as boys, if anything, withdrew them further from their father.

After his father died in 1929, Lewis wrote: 'When I saw the affection between them [a colleague and his father] … and then remembered how abominably I had treated *my* father … I was humiliated.' But his father must bear much of the blame, we feel. As his sons grew up he forced an unnatural closeness on them, allowed them no privacy, and yet refused to visit them in England. No boys could be expected to make sense of such conflicting messages.

Belsen and the Bloods

At ten years of age, only a year after his mother's death, Jack Lewis followed in Warren's footsteps to boarding school in England. It takes six chapters of Lewis's autobiographical *Surprised by Joy* to describe the trauma of his four schools, all of which were part of the British public school system, or the prep schools that fed them. When we think that this book was written some forty years after these episodes, we are amazed at the anger and outrage that shrinks the time span. We feel Lewis is having to exorcize some deep evil he senses still lodged within his spirit.

Lewis's father clearly had little idea what the system was like, or how to make informed choices within it. Warren seems to have been more outgoing and resilient than his younger brother, and more able to suppress his own unhappiness, and so the father can perhaps be forgiven for not immediately spotting the damage that was being done. So bad, though, was the first prep school (or 'concentration camp' as Lewis called it) that it was closed soon afterwards and the headmaster declared insane.

After a term at a local public school in Belfast itself, Lewis spent two years at a much better prep school in Malvern, Cherbourg School (now a girls' school, Ellerslie), while his brother attended

C.S. Lewis's dormitory at Malvern College, called 'Wyvern' in his autobiography.

Malvern College. 'Much better' is relative, of course, since it was here that he lost both what little Christian faith he had, and his innocence (Lewis gives no details). On his own admission he became vulgar and snobbish. It is a fairly consistent feature of his writings that schools come out badly – for instance in the Narnia chronicles and *The Abolition of Man*.

Lewis's greatest criticism is reserved for Malvern College, however – perhaps because he had high hopes for it. In *Surprised by Joy* it is called 'Wyvern'. His brother had just left when Lewis arrived in 1913. He describes it as being run by an in-group of socially privileged boys called 'The Bloods'; the staff seemed to have little control of anything but the academic side, homosexuality was rife, and so was the cult of the physical. Learning of any sort was looked down on, though the school possessed an excellent library, which Lewis used when he could get away from the meaningless chores thrust on him by older boys.

The only mitigation to Lewis's anger comes when he considers that most of the 'Bloods' were killed in World War I. His attitude to their deaths is ambivalent; but clearly he does not see them as the flower of Britain's youth, as contemporary English poets did. Indeed, a strong dislike of all public school types of patriotism and imperialism manifests itself in his writings, and can probably be traced back to this period. It has been suggested, even by Warren, that Malvern was no worse than other schools of its sort – an argument which could be taken to mean they were all equally as bad, which seems unlikely. What it clearly shows is that Lewis received an education despite his schooling, not because of it.

One of the redeeming features of this time was the beginnings of Lewis's friendship with Arthur Greeves, to whom Jack once wrote: 'You so often share feelings of mine which I cannot explain.' Arthur had lived near the Lewises in Belfast, but it was only by chance once vacation that Lewis suddenly discovered an identification with Arthur, not only in their love of books, reading and mythology, but also in the quality of their spiritual appetites. Arthur was from a Plymouth Brethren family, of independent means, but suffered poor health, which meant he was, unlike Lewis, if anything, overprotected. He received some training at the Slade School of Art in London, and exhibited a few times. The companionship that sprang up more than compensated for Warren's departure to Sandhurst to become an army officer, and it proved to be lifelong. Lewis's letters to Arthur, to be found in the book *They Stand Together*, give a fascinating insight into his spiritual and intellectual journey through life.

'The Great Knock'

In the end Lewis wrote to his father asking to be taken away from Malvern. Fortunately his father responded, and then did the best thing possible – he sent Lewis for private tutoring to his old headmaster at Lurgan College, W.T. Kirkpatrick, or 'The Great Knock' as he was nicknamed. Although he had retired to Bookham in Surrey by this time, Kirkpatrick's intellectual vigour and strength of character, which had made him such an able headmaster, (he became head at the age of only thirty-one) remained undimmed. His impression on Lewis was profound and longlasting, especially his totally logical approach to life. Although he clearly imparted much learning to Lewis, especially in the classics, and to a lesser extent in modern languages, it was his quality of mind that Lewis really took to and imbibed. Every statement had to be justified; every case clearly argued.

Lewis took to the new regime of study, dialectic and leisure pursuits like a duck to water. He told Arthur he had never been happier in his life. He had time to read much English literature, though Kirkpatrick never supervised nor discussed this with him, and he gradually started to enjoy walking in the countryside of southern England. By living with Kirkpatrick and his wife in a settled domestic situation, he gained some emotional stability. The collapse of domestic life he had experienced at his mother's death was now, in an unacknowledged way, being put back together. In all, he spent two years

with the Kirkpatricks, showing exceptional promise as a student, and developing habits of thinking, working and living that stayed with him the rest of his life.

Trenches and spires

Kirkpatrick wrote to Lewis's father that he could be a writer or a scholar 'but you'll not make anything else of him.' Lewis himself realized this. The natural next step therefore seemed to be to try for a scholarship to one of the Oxford colleges; so in the winter of 1916 Lewis travelled up to sit the necessary exams. Thus began an association with Oxford that lasted the rest of his life.

Lewis recalls his first entry into the city as being rather bizarre, for he took the wrong turn out of the railway station and started walking out of the city through its suburbs. Then he turned round. 'There, behind me, far away, never more beautiful since, was the fabled cluster of spires and towers.' He was duly awarded a scholarship at University College, one of the oldest of the Oxford colleges. He went up the next year, soon enlisting as an officer cadet.

Lewis did not *have* to enlist, since the Irish were exempt from compulsory military service. However, he had already decided that it was his duty, even

though, as he told Arthur at the time, 'I do not usually take much interest in the war.' He remained at Oxford until commissioned as second lieutenant in the Somerset Light Infantry. He received several postings before arriving at the frontline on his nineteenth birthday in November 1917.

By this stage of the war everyone knew how terrible trench conditions were; the earlier death-or-glory attitudes had largely evaporated. Lewis's attitude was stoical: he had expected it to be awful (unlike when he went to Malvern), and it was awful. His letters to Arthur at the time hardly mention actual conditions, but discuss the books he was somehow managing to read. In *Surprised by Joy* he briefly mentions soldierly comradeship and some of the horrors; but he felt he experienced them as if he were someone else. He caught trench fever, and then on his return to the frontline was lightly wounded in April 1918.

C.S. Lewis was demobbed in January 1919, and resumed his studies at Oxford. He tells us very little about these in his autobiography, preferring to describe the patterns of his thinking and the many new and exciting friends he made at Oxford, some of whom, such as Owen Barfield, were crucial and lifelong. The first part of his degree was in Greek and Latin; the second in philosophy.

He graduated with a double first, but competition for teaching and tutorial posts or 'fellowships' was so fierce, that Lewis was advised to get 'another arrow to his bow', by studying a third course. English language and literature was a growth area at the time, and this fitted in well with his own enthusiasm for the subject. It meant taking a three-year course in one year, including the learning of Old English (or Anglo-Saxon). He succeeded, adding a third first-class degree, a remarkable achievement, since he had had no formal academic training in English until that time.

The difficulty now remained to obtain a university teaching post. His father willingly continued to support him financially while Lewis applied for one post after another, especially in the field of philosophy, in which he finally obtained a temporary appointment. His first lecture was attended by four students! Then in 1925 C.S. Lewis applied, without much hope, for an English fellowship at Magdalen College. He was successful. This brought him a secure teaching post, rooms in college, and a reasonably generous income.

This time his first lecture overflowed with students and he had to look for a larger lecture theatre. Thus began one of the most distinguished English university teaching careers of the twentieth century.

'Home'

As an officer cadet, Lewis had made friends with a fellow Irish student, Patrick Moore. Moore's mother had separated from her husband, and she came to be near Patrick with her daughter, Maureen. Lewis and Patrick promised each other that, if either of them were to be killed in the war, the survivor would look after the other's parent. Lewis took this promise extraordinarily seriously, even before Patrick's death in the frontline.

It is not possible to discover Lewis's exact sentiments towards Mrs Moore, since he refused to disuss them in *Surprised by Joy* or at any other time. We find the clearest hints in his letters to Arthur – perhaps, since he did not want his father to know about his close involvement with Mrs Moore, Arthur was the only person he could tell anything to. Certainly when Arthur first wrote to Mrs Moore, Lewis told him he was so glad that 'the two people who matter most to me are in touch'.

Another letter to Arthur, describing a typical undergraduate day, is also revealing: after morning lectures he cycles out to Mrs Moore's at 'our own hired house', staying there to work until eleven o'clock in the evening, when he returns to college. After his first, compulsory, year in college he shared a home with Mrs Moore until her death. They lived first in digs, and then, when his father died in 1929, leaving Warren and Jack Lewis sufficient money to buy a property, in a house on Headington Quarry, called 'The Kilns'. Warren joined them there after he retired from the army in the 1930s. Maureen Moore moved away in 1940 when she married.

By all accounts, living with Mrs Moore was not easy – she gave Lewis continuous domestic chores to do; she

Magdalen College, Oxford.

seems to have had no intellectual capacity; and she complained a great deal about her health. It is hardly surprising that Lewis owns to having to wrestle with irritability and bad-temper in his domestic life. Perhaps the convert's mother in *The Screwtape Letters* owes something to her. Warren clearly thought she was silly – yet continued to live at The Kilns. Others, such as Barfield and the neighbours, liked her, Barfield describing her as a 'generous and tireless hostess'. And, when they

The chapel, Magdalen College.

could afford servants, they remained loyal to her, especially the gardener, Paxford.

Athough we could explain this continuing relationship in terms of an excessive sense of duty on Lewis's part towards his dead friend, it would seem more probable that Mrs Moore provided the parenting that Lewis desperately lacked, and a stable home from which he could live his life. Even when he had rooms in Magdalen, he would still walk out to The Kilns every afternoon, and live there during the vacation. More tellingly, perhaps, he always called where she was 'home' and 'the family', and referred to her as 'my mother', especially later when she became ill. The patience and anxiety he demonstrated at that time are those of a son towards a much-loved mother. Mrs Moore was bed-ridden from 1944, after a stroke, and died in 1951.

The Kilns itself, Lewis's home from 1930 to his death, lay in an eight-acre garden and 'is such stuff as dreams are made on', as Lewis quoted when he moved in. It was private and secluded then, with woods, a cliff, and a small lake or bathing pool. Nowadays there is much more building round it, though the house itself remains much as it always was.

Surprised by Joy

Opposite: Clive Staples Lewis in his college rooms, Magdalen College, Oxford.

In outlining some of the features of the early world of C.S. Lewis, we have mentioned several times his autobiography *Surprised by Joy*, first published in 1955. This is a special sort of autobiography, not concentrating on the historical data of his life, but tracing his spiritual journey to Christianity. In fact, there is a much earlier book, *The Pilgrim's Regress*, published only a few years after his conversion, in 1933, which also traces a spiritual journey, in a more allegorical form. It is not so directly autobiographical, but clearly its hero, John, is Lewis himself. This has never been such a popular book as *Surprised by Joy*, partly because we are not used to allegory, and partly because there is a good deal of philosophical debate in it. Lewis himself never again attempted such a straightforward allegory, even though one of his specializations was medieval allegory, and he thoroughly understood how it worked.

Hints of heaven

Before we try to trace his spiritual journey to faith, we need to establish certain key concepts in Lewis's writing and thought, the first of which is 'Desire', and its relationship with the 'Joy' of the title of the autobiography. The first thing to realize about C.S. Lewis is that beneath the intellectual scholar and philosopher, there was a powerful romantic – 'beneath' in the sense that he kept this part of himself very private until the time of his conversion, when slowly the two elements became more integrated and public.

The first section of *The Pilgrim's Regress* opens with John experiencing as a boy the law as institutional religion represented it. But his next experience, which feels like an emotional explosion, is a vision of a far-off island, and a tremendous longing for it. It is this longing or 'desire' that sets him off on his journey, much of which is spent in meeting people who either dismiss this longing and its object, or suggest false paths towards it. This is essentially the pattern that Lewis fills out in his autobiography. In the crucial first chapter he compares his earliest impressions of his parents' interest – politics, for example, and logical argument – with an innate romanticism on his part, 'the horns of elfland' as he calls them.

He then describes certain experiences as a child. He says of these 'in a sense the central story of my life is

about nothing else.' The first was a memory of a little moss garden his brother had made:

'It is difficult to find words strong enough for the sensation which came over me... it was a sensation, of course, of desire; but for what? ... It had taken only a moment of time; and in a certain sense everything else that had ever happened to me was insignificant in comparison.'

The other experiences arose from literature, but were of similar intensity. The object of desire could not be located, though part of the desire was to re-experience the sensation. So the experience was both pleasurable, and therefore joyful, and yet painful, in that it left him wanting more. He continued to experience such magic moments as a child, and then they stopped, and indeed were forgotten about, when he went to school. He calls this period 'The Dark Ages', to be followed quite suddenly by a 'reconversion' experience, bringing in the 'Renaissance' while at Malvern.

From then on he knew such desire and joy from time to time, usually connected at first with the Norse and Germanic myths and legends which had re-awakened the sensation. He found, however, he could not control its coming or going; he also discovered how different it was from pleasure, or sexuality, or the occult. The nearest experiences he read about were from the Romantic poets, in which he quickly became immersed. He finally realized two things: first, that Joy was Desire, and 'our wantings are our best havings' as he wrote to a friend; and secondly, the memory of past moments of Joy-Desire were, in fact, further experiences of Desire.

It is significant that in his book *The Problem of Pain* it is in the chapter on heaven that Lewis universalizes these experiences and puts them into their fullest Christian context. Ultimately the desire is for heaven itself, which is our soul's true home; and he assumes that everyone has such moments of immortal longing: 'All the things that have ever deeply possessed your soul have been but hints of it [heaven]'. It was the search for the object of this desire that

finally drove him towards faith.

Shadows of reality

We have just mentioned the Norse Germanic mythologies which re-awakened in him the deep sensations of joy and desire. Lewis talks of 'pure northernness' engulfing him, and it was the discovery that Arthur Greeves shared that 'northernness' that bonded them together as youths. 'Myth' is another central concept we need to examine. We use the term in its literary sense of stories which seek to explain the mysteries of life – birth, death, re-birth and the seasonal cycles, origins and creation – and which centre round gods or demi-gods, legendary heroes.

Lewis's early feeling for myth, whether Norse or Germanic, as at first, or Celtic, Greek or Roman, as later, was emotional and spiritual. There was no thought in his mind that they might be true, let alone historical. In this he was probably like most people who see myth as untrue stories, however beautiful, which we distinguish from reality.

Certainly, Lewis owns up to a sort of schizophrenia as a youth and young man: with his heart, clinging to what myth gave him; with his mind, completely rejecting any sort of truth or reality it might have. It was the realization that myth might after all be true that finally led him to a complete acceptance of Christianity. He wrote to Arthur in September 1931 that he had had 'a good long satisfying talk in which I learned a lot' with two Christian friends, about metaphor, myth and Christianity. He does not record this conversation in *Surprised by Joy*, but a significant reference to the dialogue appears in *The Pilgrim's Regress*, where John finds himself suddenly praying to God to translate 'our halting metaphor' into his 'great, unbroken speech'. This refers to something that *is* mentioned in the autobiography: Lewis's shock when an atheist friend suddenly blurted out, 'Rum thing, all that ... about the Dying God. It looks as if it had really happened once.'

Certainly this is the line that Lewis took from then on. In both *Miracles* and *The Problem of Pain* he takes a footnote to explain myth as something which *could* have occurred. But the real marrying of his old and his new attitudes is perhaps most clearly set out in his essay 'Myth became Fact', where he argues 'what flows into you from a myth is not truth but reality'. It is a perfect bridge between concrete experience and abstract ideas. This is why he complains in *The Problem of Pain* that a doctrinal explanation of The Fall never does justice to the power of the biblical myth, because only myth releases the actuality of it to the imagination and heart. Elsewhere he talks of myth as 'tasted reality', and in the science fiction stories, as well as some of the Narnia stories, he incorporates mythic elements to try to express a heightened sense of reality. For him 'the heart of Christianity is a myth which is also a fact … it is perfect myth and perfect fact'.

In a sense, then, Lewis saw Christianity as the fulfilment of paganism. Here we begin to see the Romantic nature of his Christian experience. In *The Pilgrim's Regress*, Romanticism is seen as a natural (rather than supernatural) revelation of God, and history is interspersed with such periods of revelation. One such period was that of medieval chivalry, about which he wrote so well in *The Allegory of Love*. A period nearer to hand was the Romantic revolution at the turn of the eighteenth and nineteenth centuries, which included poets such as William Wordsworth, S.T. Coleridge and John Keats. Their romanticism had two main 'witnesses': the power of the imagination to shape truth, and a love for nature. Lewis, too, sees the imagination (not the mind) as the primary organ for the reception of truth – hence the power of myth, since it speaks straight to the imagination.

His love of nature is recounted in his autobiography, coming from experiences of joy, and acting as a reminder of it. The philosophic bedrock of his Romanticism was Platonism. Although Plato was a Greek philosopher, there have always been strands of Christianity which have been able to absorb Platonism without difficulty, including two of the English writers Lewis admired most, Edmund Spenser and John

Top: Magdalen Tower from the River Cherwell.

Bottom: Addison's Walk, Oxford, where C.S. Lewis was often seen during his years at Magdalen.

Milton. At an imaginative level, Lewis had perhaps always been a Platonist: the sense that the glimpses we have of joy are gleams of a much greater, otherworldly reality, for which our soul longs and yearns, is pure Platonism, and is to be found in Thomas Traherne and William Wordsworth, two poets whom Lewis acknowledges.

Lewis's becoming a Christian 'baptized' this Platonism and gave it intellectual coherence, a process which is set out quite explicitly in *The Pilgrim's Regress*, where the opening quotation is from Plato. We are also reminded of Digory's remark in *The Last Battle*: 'It's all in Plato, all in Plato …' as they enter the other world of full reality. This world and everything in it are mere shadows and images of the perfect and

ideal world. So every human story is a shadow, a memory 'of the forgotten story in the Magician's Book.' It is this Platonism, we feel, that gives such solidity to his description of heaven, where his imagination soars, and we ourselves are caught up in rapture.

Loss of faith

Having established some key concepts in Lewis's thinking and writing, we can now more easily trace the path that led to his conversion. Conversion usually begins with little or no faith. *Surprised by Joy* sets out a loss of 'little' faith; *The Pilgrim's Regress* also does so, even if rather less clearly, in its first four books. Lewis's parents were members of the Church of Ireland, but this seems to have made little impact on him. It has been suggested that the Puritania of *The Pilgrim's Regress* must refer to the Protestantism of Ulster; but Lewis denied this, and his autobiography gives no evidence for such an assertion. He rather places his first religious awareness at his first school, where the boys were taken to a High Anglican church, and the fears of hell were laid on them, no doubt reinforced by the school regime, with its arbitrary and merciless punishments.

However, he took his faith seriously enough. But by the time he reached Malvern prep school he was caught in a legalistic struggle to 'feel' his prayers. The self-effort required was overwhelming, and he says it was with some relief that he finally dropped Christianity, under the influence of several of the school staff. This led him into several contradictions.

The schizophrenia to do with myth we have mentioned. The other was to do with his father's insistence on his being confirmed. He did not dare tell his father of his unbelief, and so 'I allowed myself to be prepared ... and confirmed ... acting a part'. In his escape from the 'fear of Christianity', and the 'No Admittance' to 'the transcendental Interferer' (his phrases) there was perhaps also a reaction to his father's invasion of privacy.

Going to Kirkpatrick was to reinforce unbelief. Later, he described the Great Knock as 'a hard satirical atheist who ... filled his house with the products of the Rationalist Press Association'. His letters to Arthur at this time confirm this. Lewis writes: 'You know, I think, that I believe in no religion. There is absolutely no proof for any of them ...' and he develops this theme over several letters. Likewise, the poetry he wrote over the next few years, later published as *Spirits in Bondage*, was similar in its philosophy to Thomas Hardy's: nature is malevolent, and if there be a God, he must be uncaring or incompetent.

The long search

Towards the end of his time with Kirkpatrick, Lewis confesses to 'intermittent wavering in my materialistic 'faith', caused by some of his reading. The Irish poet W.B. Yeats, who described himself as 'the last of the Romantics', had constructed his own private, neoplatonic mythology. What struck Lewis was that this respected, non-Christian poet actually *believed* his mythology and tried to live it out. Later, at Oxford, Lewis took the opportunity to visit Yeats, and was overwhelmed by his charisma. He mentions also the Belgian poet Maeterlinck, who, though again a non-Christian, was yet a believer in the spiritual.

But the biggest single 'bombshell' at this time to Lewis's unbelief was the discovery of the Scottish Christian writer, George Macdonald. At first Lewis seems to have played down the impact of reading one of Macdonald's prose fantasies, *Phantastes*, barely mentioning it to Arthur. But later, in his autobiography, and also in an introduction he wrote to another of Macdonald's fantasies, *Lilith*, he talks of the book 'baptizing his imagination'. It led him into the realms of myth, and yet for the first time he found the quality of 'holiness'. He had already become aware of the darker sides of Romanticism, but here was 'cool morning innocence' and 'a certain quality of Death, *good* Death'. He always acknowledged Macdonald to be his main spiritual guide and mentor, and in *The Great Divorce* the figure of Macdonald instructs him in the mysteries of heaven.

We can trace Lewis's reading of Macdonald in his letters to Arthur, as we can his reading during World War I. Without realizing it, Lewis was being attracted to Christian writers. First Macdonald, then G.K. Chesterton, with his 'commonsense' approach. Lewis has sometimes been likened to Dr Johnson in his manner, physical appearance, intellectual capacity and down-to-earthness, and sometimes to Chesterton. Certainly Lewis learned a great deal from both men's ability to express Christian truths directly and concretely.

But it was not just books that influenced Lewis; it was also people. In *The Problem of Pain* he writes 'when I first came to Oxford, I was as nearly without a moral conscience as a boy could be ... of chastity, truthfulness and self-sacrifice I thought as a baboon thinks of classical music.' He describes the effect of meeting non-Christian soldiers and students who had moral standards and ideals which were clearly not based on material self-interest. His complacency was deeply disturbed.

Two of these non-Christian students, C. Harwood and Owen Barfield, soon became converts to Anthroposophism, a set of beliefs touching somewhat on Christianity. Lewis began a 'Great War' with Barfield, by face-to-face argument and by letter, which he describes as one of the turning-points in his life. He also found Christian students he liked, one of whom, Nevill Coghill, was in the English school, and became a lifelong friend. In addition he found while reading English that the poets he most liked were all Christian!

Nevill Coghill, Fellow of Exeter College, with an undergraduate.

The Kilns, Headington Quarry, Oxford, C.S. Lewis's home for many years.

On the other hand there were opposing forces, especially the new psychology, which dismissed the spiritual; and several people to whose spirituality he took the strongest dislike. But his 'war' with Barfield showed him that just because something was the latest trend did not make it any more likely. The journey to faith was beginning.

The Grand Canyon

In *The Pilgrim's Regress* John finally comes to an enormous chasm right across his road. He has come as far as he can by his own efforts, and those of his companion, Virtue. He meets a figure called Mother Kirk (the Christian gospel) who offers to carry him down one side of this chasm, or 'Grand Canyon', and up the other. He refuses, and seeks his own way down by journeying along northwards and then southwards. Finally, trapped on a narrow ledge, he is confronted by Christ himself, and has to surrender himself to Christ's ways of death to self, and rising to new life through spiritual baptism.

The parallel account of his conversion in *Surprised by Joy*, written many years after, makes a similar two-stage process, but significantly changes the details. Here the first stage is coming to God, and thus adopting a theistic position. The second stage is realizing who Christ is, and thus embracing Christianity. The stress here is on the first stage, whereas in the *Regress* it is more on the second.

Lewis moved from Idealism, with no idea of a personal God, to Pantheism, the idea of an impersonal God in everything, a stance that a number of Romantics adopted. From there he edged slowly to Theism. He sees it as a natural road, and was surprised at the time that there were so few other seekers. He suggests it may have been because Idealism was no longer in fashion; but more likely it was because there are so few seekers – certainly few intellectual seekers – who also have a tremendous desire for spiritual fulfilment.

Most of this took place during the later 1920s, with Lewis secure in his teaching post. He describes some of the temptations of the *dolce vita* of an Oxford don's life in the characters of Mr Sensible, the cultured hedonist or Epicurean, and Mr Broad, the liberal, broad-minded churchman, in *The Pilgrim's Regress*. He was also still seeking to be a poet, working on a long poem, *Dymer*, a sort of medieval fantasy epic. When published it attracted little attention.

What strikes us in Lewis's accounts of his move towards faith are the metaphors of catching and being caught. He talks of the angler; of chess-playing; of cat and mouse. In human terms, he expresses it in *Voyage to Venus* as the fear of being drawn into something; in theological terms, in *The Problem of Pain*, the language is of 'election', that is, being chosen, even pursued, by God's grace. God is the divine chess-player making the good moves against Lewis, the beginner.

The paradox of 'calling' yet 'being called' is beautifully portrayed in the Narnia books *The Silver Chair* and *The Horse and his Boy*. Lewis, at one moment, felt he had a perfectly free choice, yet was bound to make only *one* choice. So ultimately his 'search' for truth became God's 'search' for him. As he puts it in his autobiography, one might as well talk about the 'mouse's search for the cat'! So in the Trinity term of 1929, he writes in the now famous words: 'I gave in and admitted that God was God, and knelt and prayed...'

The Pilgrim's Regress

Lewis's final move to Christianity is

much less dramatically portrayed in his autobiography. In fact his description of the day he went to Whipsnade Zoo in Warren's motorbike sidecar not a Christian and returned as one seems almost an anti-climax, just as is his conclusion about joy: 'to tell you the truth the subject has lost nearly all interest for me'. For he had come home and found the true source of joy.

In fact, we get perhaps a better picture in his letters to Arthur, which are very frequent and full over the period 1929–31. In them we see the beginnings of a real religious consciousness, with genuine spiritual insights; we see him looking at his moral state (and being horrified at the pride he found in himself); we see him trying to throw off old habits of temper and scepticism. He also writes of his reading of the German mystic Boehme: 'I wish to record that it has been the biggest shaking up I've got since I first read *Phantastes* ... it's a real book, i.e. it's not like a book at all, but like a thunderclap.' It gave him new insights into God as creator and of the incarnation. But it was the meaning of redemption that proved the biggest sticking point, and, as we have already seen, he explains to Arthur how his talk on true myth with two Christian friends, Tolkien and Dyson, slotted this into place for him.

Converts usually take strong attitudes and find ways to express these. For Lewis, the immediate way was to write *The Pilgrim's Regress* and to use it, like Bunyan, to demonstrate not only the true way, but also the false pilgrims. On the journey to faith John discovers their falsity only with difficulty. But John, unlike Christian in *Pilgrim's Progress*, has to make a journey back, when he sees truly; falsities are seen as horrors, not as attractions. On the return also comes the integration of the emotional and intellectual sides of his nature through various ordeals.

Remarkably, he wrote the book in two weeks, giving it to Arthur to comment on. Arthur was not happy about the style of some of the learned references. While Lewis changed a few things, we are still left with a prose work that lacks the qualities of a novel, without quite being a comprehensible

C.S. Lewis's brother, Warren.

argument for Christianity. Nevertheless, it is overneglected, and shows the way Lewis was to develop as a writer of fiction and as a defender of the rationality and sense of Christianity. He also shows his power to demolish opposition; not just false philosophies, but especially liberal theology. To the very end of his life he abhorred the watering-down he saw in liberal theology, and his language stayed as intense as ever. His picture of the modernist bishop returning to hell, in *The Great Divorce*, is not only unforgettable but surprisingly topical. Finally, Lewis discovered his brother had also, in a quiet way, found his own way back to faith, and they were able thus to enjoy a deeper fellowship as Warren came to live at The Kilns.

The Inklings

The Radcliffe Camera, Oxford.

Twice weekly

Writing to a publisher, Lewis said:
'My happiest hours are often spent with three or four old friends in old clothes tramping together and putting up in small pubs – or else sitting up till the small hours in someone's college rooms, talking nonsense, poetry, theology, metaphysics over beer, tea and pipes. There's no sound I like better than adult male laughter.'

So who were these 'old friends'? We have already mentioned Owen Barfield. Unfortunately, Barfield was not able to stay in Oxford on entering the legal profession, but he kept up his friendship with Lewis, visiting when he could. Later he became one of the two trustees of Lewis's estate. We have also met Arthur Greeves, but he rarely visited Oxford, and therefore does not enter directly the next stage of Lewis's world.

Lewis, however, continued to tell Arthur of his Oxford friends. For instance, in 1930 he met Hugo Dyson, a lecturer at Reading University, only a short train journey away. He writes of his first impressions: 'He is a man who really loves truth: a philosopher and a religious man ...' and then describes the curious blend of deadly serious conversation and uproarious laughter that was such a feature of Lewis's style. It was Dyson who was one of the people who helped Lewis to see that myth could be true, and so provided the breakthrough for him to Christianity.

The other friend who helped in this was J.R.R. Tolkien, easily the best known of Lewis's friends at this time. Lewis had first met Tolkien at English faculty meetings and had quite liked him from the start. Tolkien was an Old English specialist who soon achieved professorial status. He was also a committed Roman Catholic. After Lewis's conversion, their friendship blossomed, and, despite Tolkien's being a married man, there were many midnight talks. In 1933 Tolkien showed Lewis the manuscript of *The Hobbit.* Lewis told Arthur: 'Reading (it) has been uncanny – it is so exactly like what we would both have longed to write (or read) in 1916...' Tolkien also ran a club, the 'Kolbitars' (an Old Norse term for

Interior of the Eagle and Child public house, Oxford, where Lewis and his friends often met.

those who sit round fires), which was devoted to reading Old Norse myths and legends in the original. Although Lewis had not learned the language, he nevertheless attended avidly.

Another club or society which Lewis attended at this time was called 'The Inklings'. It had been started by a student, for the purpose of members' listening to each others' writings. It was a formal society, with minutes being kept, but it dissolved when its founder left Oxford in 1933. However, the name revived informally at some stage over the next few years round a group of friends who met weekly in Lewis's rooms in Magdalen New Buildings – rooms he occupied for thirty years. Their purpose was to read to each other what they had been writing, talk about it, and then discuss more generally any topic that interested them.

Humphrey Carpenter traces the history of this group in his excellent book *The Inklings*. He suggests the group was for encouraging one another, rather than to be a creative writing group as such; but it would be difficult to say what else bound them together. A common disagreement with modernist literature; a commitment to religious truth; a love for mythology have all been suggested. A more human reason would be Lewis's capacity for male friendship and his personal magnetism.

The group was certainly flourishing by 1938, and several attempts have been made to reconstruct a Thursday evening in Lewis's shabby rooms. After a youthful zest for buying well-bound new books, Lewis seems to have gone in for shabby books, or ones from his father's library, actually preferring to use the books in the Bodleian, the main university library. His furniture was equally shabby, as was The Kilns later, after Mrs Moore became bedridden. Meetings of the Inklings apparently began between nine o'clock and ten-thirty, and would continue till the small hours. It was at such meetings that Tolkien read some of *The Lord of the Rings* and Lewis some of his science fiction and apologetics, though hardly any of the Narnia stories, for the Thursday evenings petered out in the autumn of 1949. Some older members had drop-

Professor J.R.R. Tolkien, author of *The Lord of the Rings*, in his study at Merton College, Oxford.

ped out by that time, and not all the new ones were so committed or in tune with each other.

The Inklings also used to drink beer together on Tuesday mornings at an Oxford pub officially called 'The Eagle and Child', but affectionately known as 'The Bird and Baby'. It stands in St Giles, and is now somewhat of a mecca for Lewis aficionados. These were totally informal gatherings for chat and fellowship. Later they moved to another pub called 'The Lamb and Flag', and sometimes they went out to a nearby village inn, 'The Trout' at Godstow. This gathering changed to a Monday when Lewis received a Cambridge professorship in 1954, the group usually adjourning to see Lewis off to his train. This continued until his death in 1963, though it was never formally referred to as the Inklings after the Thursday evenings finished.

C.S. Lewis

Recently, efforts have been made to see the Inklings as a highly significant group. The people in it certainly were, and their friendships together were significant to them personally. But to try to see them as 'The Christian Romantics' or 'Romantic theologians' is to put too formal a categorization on them. Like an earlier Oxford grouping, 'The Holy Club', to which the Wesleys belonged, we could perhaps say that people were brought together in committed friendship and fellowship, and out of that was created something far beyond what the group meant or foresaw for itself.

'Ugly as a chimpanzee'

Two people not mentioned so far in connection with the Inklings are Charles Williams and Lewis's brother, Warren. Although not an academic, Warren keenly enjoyed intellectual discussion and came to act as host for the Inklings. He often worked in Lewis's rooms at college, either assisting Jack or pursuing his own research in French history, which became his particular published interest. We could also mention here some of the better known post-war Inklings: Tolkien's son, Christopher, and J.A.W. Bennett, who later succeeded Lewis as professor at Cambridge. The scholar Lord David Cecil and the writer John Wain also attended at times.

But it was Charles Williams who had the greatest influence on Lewis, who said he owed everything to him and called him his 'friend of friends'. They seemed to be on exactly the same spiritual wave-length. Writing to Arthur, Lewis described him as 'of humble origin (there are still traces of cockney in his voice), ugly as a chimpanzee but so radiant (he emanates more *love* than any man I have ever known) that as soon as he begins talking ... he looks like an angel.' This electrifying quality of Williams' speaking was witnessed to by many others, including those who heard him lecture at Oxford. Women, it seems, were particularly attracted by these qualities, but clearly Lewis responded equally enthusiastically.

Lewis had first come across Williams in 1936, when reading one of his early novels, *The Place of the Lion*. At that time there was a brief exchange of letters, as Williams was on the editorial staff of the Oxford University Press in London, which was publishing Lewis's *The Allegory of Love*. At the beginning of World War II, the press evacuated back to Oxford, and Williams with it. Immediately he was pressed into the Inklings, where he seemed to fit at once. Lewis described their 'Bird and Baby' talk as 'so fast and furious that the company thinks we're talking bawdy when in fact we're very likely talking theology'.

Although Williams had no formal qualifications, Lewis managed to get him on to the English department lecture programme, to teach a course on Milton. The lectures were quite unique, and influenced Lewis in his book *A Preface to Paradise Lost*, which he was writing at the time. But perhaps the greatest literary influence on Lewis was through Williams's fantasy novels —

where the ordinary world is somehow invaded by outside forces. As Lewis claims in his essay on 'The Novels of Charles Williams', illumination is given both on the quality of our everyday lives and also on the spiritual forces of good and evil around us. The change in Lewis's own science fiction, seen in his novel *That Hideous Strength*, can be directly attributed to Williams's fiction. Theologically, too, Williams counteracted Lewis's extreme rationality in his apologetics – Williams showed him that theology contains paradoxes that neither can nor should be resolved logically.

Although Williams was only ten years older than Lewis, he never enjoyed good health. He died quite suddenly in 1945. As a tribute to his friend, Lewis edited the Arthurian epic Williams had been engaged in writing for many years, adding an essay to it; he also contributed to what in effect was the Inklings' homage, *Essays Presented to Charles Williams*, which the Oxford University Press published soon after.

Talks and apologies

In a letter to Arthur around the time of his conversion, Lewis wrote:
'From the age of sixteen onwards I had one single ambition, from which I never wavered, in the prosecution of which I spent every ounce I could, on which I really and deliberately staked my whole contentment: and I recognize myself as having unmistakeably failed in it.'

He was trying to console Arthur at the time and may have exaggerated the sense of his own failure as a poet. It would seem, however, that the sense of failure acted to produce a right sort of humility, for never at any later time does the thought of literary fame touch him, or its actuality. He even used to throw away copies of his own books sent to him by his publishers, as well as many of his original manuscripts.

When World War II began, Lewis's fame was still limited to the academic world, and was largely due to his *Allegory of Love* and his controversy with Professor Tillyard of Cambridge, published as *The Personal Heresy* in 1939. There was nothing to indicate the sudden rise to fame which occurred during the war, and which has continued unabated ever since. The fame needs to be seen coming in two waves: the first, wartime, wave has to do with his defence of orthodox Christianity (technically called 'apologetics') against modern unbelief, both secular and theological; the second, in the 1950s, is associated with his children's stories. There is no obvious link between them unless we remember Lewis's twofold nature: the rational, logical philosopher; and the romantic lover of myth and 'the thorns of elfland'. In much of his writing we find one side or the other; in some we have both.

In 1939 Geoffrey Bles, a small publishing company, decided to create 'The Christian Challenge' series of books and Lewis was asked to contribute a volume on suffering. Although *The Pilgrim's Regress* had sold few copies, it had gained admirers, and it was through one of these that the invitation came. Lewis had the intellectual stimulus of the Inklings while writing *The Problem of Pain*, as he decided to call the new book. 'A little thing', he told Arthur, but it was an immediate success. Indeed, by 1974 it had gone through twenty hard-cover printings alone, and continues to be one of his best-sellers.

On first appearance, Lewis struck many people as a 'hale and hearty' type of man, very forceful, but perhaps not oversensitive to suffering or weakness. But beneath the appearance there was, in fact, a real vulnerability. He confesses to Arthur many times of great unhappiness, some of which was no doubt occasioned by Mrs Moore, though he had, of course, suffered much as a child. The clearest example of his capacity to suffer came later, in the grief experienced on the death of his wife.

But even if we have established a sympathy in Lewis for his subject matter, his approach to it in the book seems immediately academic and philosophical. The method is typical of him: a ground-clearing operation first, followed by foundation laying, and only then a building up of the main argument. A reader has to wait some time before he feels he is getting some

The Eagle and Child pub, St Giles', Oxford.

C.S. Lewis
Surprised
by Joy

answers. Lewis holds attention by giving us confidence that answers will be forthcoming, but the difficulties are real and we need patience. The central theme does not emerge until chapter six: that self-surrender to the will of God is vital, and only when we understand this can we see any purpose in suffering. In this book, some of Lewis's best writing occurs when he moves away from the strictly logical to paint a picture of man before the fall, or to describe the condition of hell. We feel here that his imagination transforms the logic to present powerful statements, and to set our hearts as well as our minds on God's redemptive purposes, and the hope of heaven.

Lewis's emergence as a champion of orthodox Christianity, during World War II, is not quite as coincidental as it might appear. Lewis saw his mission as a defender in a spiritual warfare going on in contemporary culture, and that his 'war service' was literally to fight for truth. This is what led him, for example, to trek round Royal Air Force camps up and down the United Kingdom giving talks on Christianity to servicemen. But the war also brought a new openness to religion, and Christian publishers found ready markets for their books. Peacetime complacencies were shattered, and the foundations of people's lives were deeply disturbed.

Mere Christianity

It was this new openness that led the B.B.C. (British Broadcasting Corporation) to ask Lewis to broadcast for them, following the success of *The Problem of Pain*. Lewis immediately agreed, though the medium of radio was new to him. The first series was broadcast weekly live in the autumn of 1941. It attracted an immediate response of letters, most of which Lewis felt it his moral duty to reply to. In fact, the first series consisted of two parts: the first seeking to establish that we have an innate sense of law, of right and wrong, and that we need to have a belief in God for that sense to take on any real meaning. The second was to establish the main belief of Christianity: that Jesus was God in man – a stupendous

claim about which we have to do something.

Bles published the talks the next year, at which time Lewis undertook a second radio series, this time pre-recorded, entitled 'Christian Behaviour'. A third series followed in 1944, 'Beyond Personality', which deals with what it is to be a Christian and in relationship with God. The three resulting books were finally combined into one in 1952 as *Mere Christianity*, a phrase taken from the seventeenth-century Christian writer, Richard Baxter, and meaning the basic form and beliefs of Christianity accepted by orthodox believers of all traditions and denominations.

Also in 1942 probably Lewis's most famous book appeared, *The Screwtape Letters*, having first been serialized in a religious journal. It is the one book Lewis stated he did *not* enjoy writing, since imagining what one devil might write to another got right inside him and made him feel all 'gritty'. For all that, the book has immense verve and a weird sort of humour, and again, immediately took hold of the public.

Although Lewis said the idea came to him suddenly in 1940, we can trace origins for it. For example, while at Bookham, he wrote to Arthur Greeves: 'I wonder what a book called *Letters from Hell* ... would be like?' This book, when obtained, was a disappointment, a sort of romantic novel. Another book he read, Stephen McKenna's *Confessions of a Well-Meaning Woman* (1922) has been suggested as another genesis. Certainly, the black-and-white polarities of hell and heaven fitted in well with Lewis's style of arguing and imagining, as they did later in *The Great Divorce* (1945), which paints the other side of the picture, the outlook from heaven. These are both much more imaginative, fictional types of work, less obviously intellectual, representing the other strand of his apologetic work: the depiction of certain spiritual states, especially the joys of the heavenly and the miseries of the hellish.

During this period, there existed at Oxford a very lively and flourishing debating society called the Socratic Club, of which Lewis was president. It became a forum for arguments for and against religion, Lewis himself speaking some eleven times in main speeches, as well as consistently taking part in the debate from the floor. In this way, many generations of students were able to hear Lewis at his philosophical, logical best. The only time he seems to have been worsted was in 1947 by a professional philosopher, G.E.M. Anscombe – to make it worse for Lewis, she was a woman and a Catholic – he still had doubts about the intellectual capacities of both categories.

Lewis had been writing and talking a lot about the miraculous at this time. To him, Christianity was nothing if not supernatural, and he felt he was up against both materialists and liberal theologians who *a priori* dismissed miracles as 'unhistorical' and 'unscientific'. Thus Lewis's defence was strategic. He endeavours to show they are neither unhistorical nor unscientific, and thus Christianity *is* credible. It has been suggested that after Lewis's 'defeat' at the hands of Miss Anscombe, he retired from active apologetics. Certainly, he modified that particular chapter in *Miracles*, but the constant stream of papers and talks that he gave for the rest of his life hardly suggests a defeated man. Lewis was not the sort of person to be put off by one fall in the cut-and-thrust of academic debate.

One last book needs to be mentioned here, *The Abolition of Man* (1947). This is a book perhaps more popular in the United States than in Britain; Walter Hooper, the other Lewis trustee, writes of it: 'This ... is perhaps the most important book Lewis ever wrote and almost certainly the finest defence of the Moral Law there is.' It starts as an attack on the teaching of English at secondary school level, but it goes on to broaden into a warning about the possible loss of values in our society through sceptical approaches to moral statements of truth, value and worth, and their reduction to subjective states. Such a warning was indeed prophetic, and we might feel the confusion of values both in our schools and in our society is exactly what Lewis predicted. The book is not specifically Christian apologetic, appealing to the 'Tao' of an-

The roofs of Brasenose College and Exeter College, Oxford.

cient Eastern wisdom as much as to Greek and Christian concepts.

All this fame, of course, brought Lewis many invitations to speak, preach and write articles. Much of what he produced for these was of an apologetic nature, sometimes, but not always, on themes covered by the books. A few of these pieces were collected together before his death, for example in *They asked for a Paper* (1962), but mostly they have been gathered since by Walter Hooper and published by Collins, in the United Kingdom and Macmillan in the United States. Two of his best collections of essays are *God in the Dock*, which takes its title from an address on the difficulties of presenting the Christian gospel to modern unbelievers; and *Screwtape Proposes a Toast*, containing two marvellous war-time sermons – 'Transposition' and 'The Weight of Glory', the latter preached to a packed Oxford congregation. Not naturally a preacher, these show in Lewis an inspiration worthy of the best.

PAN-Books

VOYAGE TO VENUS
(PERELANDRA)
C. S. Lewis

Novel of Strange Adventure on Another World
by Author of Out of the Silent Planet 2'

Other Worlds

Science fiction

Miracles, then, was the last of Lewis's major apologetic works – last not because of any uncertainty about the possibilities of defending Christianity as a rational religion, but because he had said all he wanted to say in that way. He possibly felt also that his arguments were getting too complex and over-academic for the average man in the street, for whom, after all, he was primarily writing. His Royal Air Force talks had convinced him of the vital necessity for simple language.

But for the direction which his writing took in the 1950s, and the second 'wave' of fame, we need to look back to 1937, the year Lewis started to write science fiction, with *Out of the Silent Planet*. Oxford dons have been known to write such books for light relief, but Lewis's purposes were quite other. Although his first literary ambition had been poetry, he had had a long childhood apprenticeship in prose, writing about an imaginary 'Animal Land', which later became combined with Warren's literary endeavours in 'Boxen'.

In adolescence he developed an appetite for science fiction, and in his autobiography he suggests that his own science fiction was an exorcism of his 'lust' and the 'coarseness and eagerness of his original appetite'. He was by no means a high-brow reader as he grew older. As his letters to Arthur Greeves show, he delighted in reading and re-reading such Victorian favourites as Sir Walter Scott, Wilkie Collins and Rider Haggard. H.G. Wells he much admired, but the book which really showed him the spiritual possibilities of the science fiction genre was David Lindsay's *A Voyage to Arcturus*, a strange allegorical fantasy set on a planet of another universe.

Lewis's own science fiction certainly explores the spiritual possibilities of the form, more or less disregarding the science, though not from ignorance.

Lewis was able to discuss scientific ideas quite intelligently, even without a formal training, and indirectly he attacks ideas of such contemporary scientists as Professor J.B.S. Haldane, especially as they are expressed by one of his characters, Weston.

In *Out of the Silent Planet*, the discussion of such ideas starts very cautiously, however. The hero, Ransom, is kidnapped by Weston and his associate, Devine, and finally reaches Malacandra (Mars) where he is to be offered up as some sort of 'ransom' so that Weston and Devine can exploit the planet's gold. Ransom himself fears the worst, having imbibed the hitherto current science fiction philosophy that humans are better than aliens, and is amazed to discover that the strange inhabitants of the planet are unfallen beings, who mean good to him, and are ruled over by 'Oyarsa', or angelic beings, who serve 'Maleldil', or God. Ransom finally has his eyes opened to the fact that only Earth has fallen, ruled over by an evil Oyarsa (Satan), and is thus silent, unable to communicate with the rest of the spiritual universe. Weston and Devine receive no such enlightenment. The plot unfolds logically and simply; the idea is surprising, though the characterization and dialogue are somewhat wooden – difficulties Lewis had in *The Pilgrim's Regress*, his only previous prose fiction work.

The next science fiction is very much more successful all round, and remained Lewis's favourite: *Perelandra* (1943), later reprinted as *Voyage to Venus*. Lewis was also writing on 'Paradise Lost' at the time, and listening to Williams's lectures. He had the Inklings to read the novel to, so it is not surprising that its ideas are far more developed, and that both characterization and plot are more complex. Again, Ransom features centrally, and Weston is the villain – this time meeting a gruesome death as he is taken over by evil forces, becoming the 'Unman'.

Someone has called the novel 'Paradise Retained', for the parallels with Milton's epic are close. Venus is the new Eden, with an unfallen Eve. As with Milton, the woman is separated from her man and is tempted, but this time resists the temptation. Paradise is thus assured for her and her descendants.

As we saw with *The Problem of Pain*, Lewis is very good at imagining man before the Fall – much better than Milton. He also avoids Milton's difficulty of making the devil perhaps too attractive, by putting the temptation into the mouth of the Unman – an obviously gruesome being. The temptations are basically the same as Milton's, which are ultimately those of the Genesis account: pride, questioning God's decree, rebellion against hierarchy, and vanity. The temptation scenes are very long and we get a real sense of touch-and-go with them. Like Ransom, we look on, almost helplessly, forgetting, as he does, God's grace given to us all at such moments. The novel ends in a rapture of Platonic idealism, where Greek myth and Christian truth merge in a hymn of joy.

The last fiction, *That Hideous Strength* (1945), is very different, and owes a lot to Williams's influence. It is set, as with Williams's novels, in England in the not-too-distant future. Under the guise of technological advance led by Devine, satanic forces infiltrate the universities and the state apparatus. The spiritual forces of good centre round a much wiser Ransom, but the myth of Merlin returned to life is also brought in. Confusion is finally brought on the evil forces, and they are swallowed up in an earthquake.

All this sounds rather unlikely, and the novel does lack a certain credibility all the way through. Merlin and the animals appear particularly ridiculous. Yet for all its very obvious faults, it is by far the most ambitious of the novels and, if anything, fails through trying to say too much. The most successful element is the tracing of the progress of the 'modern' young couple, Mark and Jane Studdock, as they learn the realities of spiritual warfare and the need to make black and white choices. By telling the

The chapel, Magdalen College, Oxford.

story through their perceptions, Lewis is able to open up to us the nature of human fallenness and the possibilities of grace.

Aslan

Lewis once remarked that he did not enjoy the company of small children. Elsewhere he explained this in terms of shyness. Nor did he have any of his own children; he was not even an uncle, though he was a godfather. By the time he did 'inherit' stepchildren, he had already written the Narnia stories. Writing academic or theological books, even science fiction, with no children around hardly seems a likely preparation for a writer whose stories vie with those of Tolkien and Enid Blyton for top sales. We should remember, perhaps, another Oxford don who was single – Lewis Carroll – but even he had in mind a child to whom to tell the Alice stories. We must look elsewhere for explanations.

In fact, we must look back to Lewis's childhood reading and to the moments of joy and desire that came through such reading. In a sense it was for 'the child within' that Lewis wrote, creating the sort of stories he would have liked as a child. Lewis much preferred to read or re-read children's books than read light adult fiction, E. Nesbit, Beatrix Potter and *The Wind in the Willows* being favourites.

The actual writing of the seven Narnia stories occurred over a comparatively short space of time between 1949

'The rabble ... began to drag the bound and muzzled Lion to the Stone Table, some pulling and some pushing.' An illustration from *The Lion, The Witch and the Wardrobe*.

and 1953. As we have said, Lewis read the first book, *The Lion, the Witch and the Wardrobe*, to the Inklings before they dissolved. He had a rather mixed reception, Tolkien not liking it at all. This seems surprising at first, since *The Hobbit* would appear to have obvious affinities. But *The Hobbit* had grown out of years of Tolkien's constructing an imaginary world, for which he had created myths, legends, histories and a geography, as well as several languages. There was none of this for Lewis; Narnia suddenly appeared. Tolkien felt it was somehow cheating, and not the way the secondary world of fantasy ought to work. Also, Tolkien took a scholar's interest in his world; Lewis did not – it came from the depths of his imagination, often emerging from it in the form of vivid and haunting images.

There is something of a debate about the order in which the Narnia books ought to be read. The Penguin editions previously stated the 'correct' order as *The Lion, the Witch and the Wardrobe*, followed by *Prince Caspian*, then *The Voyage of the Dawn Treader*, *The Silver Chair*, *The Horse and his Boy*, and finally *The Magician's Nephew* and *The Last Battle*. This represents the original order of publication by Geoffrey Bles and The Bodley Head, who brought them out more or less one

a year from 1950 to 1956. However, Walter Hooper, in his *Past Watchful Dragons*, argues we should read them in the order of Narnian time, which means starting at the beginning of Narnia in *The Magician's Nephew*, then working through *The Lion, the Witch and the Wardrobe*, *The Horse and his Boy*, *Prince Caspian*, *The Voyage of the Dawn Treader*, *The Silver Chair*, and finishing with the ending of Narnia in *The Last Battle*. At first sight this seems a completely different order, but really it is only the order of *The Magician's Nephew* we need to argue about. (The current Penguin edition adopts this order.)

It is also interesting to note how the illustrator, Pauline Baynes, quite a young and inexperienced artist to start with, developed her own style through the series. Lewis maintained a good working relationship with her throughout. The American paperback editions (by Macmillan) lack many of her illustrations, and their absence is very apparent.

Whatever the merits of Hooper's argument, we shall in fact discuss the books in their order of publication. We have mentioned various images which often gave shape to the story which followed. One such image was of 'a Faun carrying an umbrella and parcels in a snowy wood'. Lewis had had this image ever since he was sixteen. This image may have been rekindled reading a children's story called *The Wood that Time Forgot*, by one of his former students, Roger Lancelyn Green, who went on to become one of Lewis's biographers and a noted re-teller of myths and legends for children. Another image was of a queen on a sledge, perhaps inspired by Hans Christian Andersen's story 'The Snow Queen'.

But it was the image of a lion, recurring in Lewis's dreams, some of them terrifying, that sparked the first book into life. The lion is a natural symbol for royalty, and in *The Great Divorce* we find wonderful biblical images of lions playing in heaven. Lions are also basically untameable, and right through the books the refrain is 'Aslan is not a tame lion'. In *The Problem of Pain* Lewis had discussed tame animals, occasioning some controversy as to whether they were 'better' than wild ones. In Narnia he achieves a solution, by making some animals talk, which means they are civilized yet free.

The creation of Aslan was a stroke of genius, and provided the unifying dynamic for the six books to follow as well as the focus of spiritual insight. Children are naturally attracted to animal stories. In Aslan we have more than an animal, and yet in him are all the factors that can attract children: he is other than grown-ups, yet powerful, more powerful than the witch; he is noble, yet relates to the children with courtesy, so raising them in importance; and yes, he is cuddly, but in a quite profound way of total love and spiritual warmth, again in contrast to the witch, and in a way which includes playfulness and gentleness. And he lays down his life. Lewis's treatment of this in terms of 'deep magic' and 'a yet deeper magic' is bold and imaginative, and provides genuine tragic dimensions not only for young children, but for all readers who recognize how much evil can be released through human weakness, and how much loving sacrifice is often needed to redeem it.

Prince Caspian could be seen as a sequel story; it is a 'return', and it is placed within a year of the four children's first Narnian adventure. Yet, as with the first story, time confusion is immediately obvious. Narnian time exists almost independently of earth time; in the one year on earth, the golden age of Old Narnia has passed away; descendants of other 'sons of Adam' have invaded and established a kingdom of New Narnia. The children are recalled to help the rightful heir to *this* dynasty gain his crown. There are perhaps faint echoes of English history; the old England of the Anglo-Saxons is replaced by the new kingdom of the Normans. There is no question of going back on history.

But underneath the old and the new is a deeper concept of 'the true Narnia', first set out in *That Hideous Strength* as 'the true Logres', an idea that could be traced back to Charles Williams. As with *That Hideous Strength*, the book ends in a riot of mythic revelry, Christ-

ian joy combining with pagan profusion – with a few cheeky remarks about schools that children would love.

The Voyage of the Dawn Treader is hardly a sequel to this, for only the two younger children are 'allowed' back to Narnia, this time with their grim cousin Eustace. The book has memorable moments – Eustace's transformation into dragon, and the final mysterious chapters where they approach the world's edge (echoing William Morris's *The Well at the World's End*). But the book is a bit of a mixed bag, with bathos mixed with sublimity and with too many literary borrowings for any unity of tone.

If *The Voyage of the Dawn Treader* is a journey over the seas, *The Silver Chair* is one underground. There is a great feeling of fairy story and medieval fantasy to it, with patterns of temptations, of warnings not heeded, of giants and monsters. But also there are strands of Rider Haggard, Jules Verne, Jonathan Swift's *Gulliver's Travels*, and George Macdonald. The plot line is much stronger than in *The Voyage of the Dawn Treader*, however, and is able to fuse together these disparate elements much more successfully.

Just as Reepicheep, the valiant mouse, enlivens *The Voyage of the Dawn Treader*, so Puddleglum, the lugubrious 'marsh-wiggle', enlivens this book. The Lewis's gardener-cum-cook, Paxford, provided the model. The queen's temptation of the captive prince is not unlike Weston's tempting of the lady in *Perelandra*. Lewis's imagination is not creating an entirely new world, but re-forming his own adult reading and thinking into a new texture for children – but of course, not just for children, since we as adults have adult truth mediated to us in new ways too.

The Horse and his Boy takes us back to Old Narnia, but this time there are no earth children involved. The boy is a kidnapped prince from one of the Narnian lands; the horse is a kidnapped talking horse. A lot is made here of *free* Narnia; Aslan intervenes to guide them back. It is much more story as sheer story, with the favourite comedy device of the lost twin found to give it a happy ending.

C.S. Lewis; a characteristic pose.

a stature that the others do not quite attain. If you have read it once, it is almost unbearably sad to read it again. It is a painful, threatening book, because good seems to be defeated; Narnia is tricked out of its heritage, and the false god Tash, seen for the first time properly in *The Horse and his Boy*, literally comes into Narnia to assume power.

The strength of evil, so well portrayed in *That Hideous Strength*, is simply and starkly shown, as is human (and dwarvish) cunning and treachery. Yet the moment of defeat – at a stable door, significantly – becomes the moment of Aslan's judgement. The book suddenly takes on eschatological dimensions, as the end of Narnia comes suddenly upon us. And then, out of misery, the revelation of a 'truer' Narnia is shown us 'higher up and deeper in', and the perfect forms of Platonism become fused with the Paradise of 'new heavens and a new earth'.

It comes as a shock to realize that the end of Narnia for the children was also the end of their earthly life, for they have been killed in a railway accident. So the end of the book really does take us up into heaven itself. Eternal life is seen as a story, and 'now at last they were beginning chapter one of the great story'. This is an incredibly bold stroke for what is often a very safe world of writing (that is, for children), and it is amazing that what starts with something so petty and miserable can finish on such a glorious and powerful note.

Allegory or fantasy?

We should consider what Lewis was actually doing in creating this imaginative world of Narnia, as well as the readership he intended. Was it for children that he wrote, and was it to teach them valuable truths about Christianity?

We usually call literature that sets out to teach in a systematic way didactic. One type of didactic writing is allegory, such as Lewis's *The Pilgrim's Regress*, or its great predecessor, Bunyan's *Pilgrim's Progress*. As we have seen, in his allegory Lewis shows not only how he came to faith, but also what is false about each of the beliefs and attitudes he encountered on the way. However, when giving a talk on the Narnia stories

The last two books are of beginnings and ends, and their whole tone is far more serious. *The Magician's Nephew* is set in E. Nesbit's England, but before Narnia is created. The human interest is in Digory's mother dying. The mythic interest is of dying and newly-born worlds; Malacandra and Perelandra are re-cast. But this time the dying world is evil, and Jadis, its empress, finds her way, through the two children of the story, into the world of Narnia as Aslan is creating it. Aslan is finally revealed as creator, and with the power to comprehend evil and contain it in his new world. Mythic elements of the Paradise garden come in; it is an apple from this garden that finally heals Digory's mother. Like *That Hideous Strength*, it is perhaps too ambitious, trying to do and say too much, so that ultimately nothing is said quite clearly enough.

This cannot be said for *The Last Battle*, which was awarded the Carnegie Award – a prestigious English award for the best children's book of the year. It has been argued that it was really awarded for the whole series; but it could just as well be argued that this is the best book of the series, and achieves to the Library Association in 1952, entitled 'On Three Ways of Writing for Children', Lewis rejects any such didactic purpose for them. Rather, he wanted a form of literature where he could leave things out, to check the 'expository demon in me'.

At most we could say that where Lewis echoes allegorical writers such as Bunyan or Swift, then his stories do take on allegorical possibilities. For example, one popular allegorical form is the journey or the voyage (paralleling our journey through life), and in *The Voyage of the Dawn Treader*, some of the incidents *could* be interpreted allegorically; as could *The Horse and his Boy* which *could* be seen to parallel Lewis's own spiritual journey. But they do not *need* to be read like this at all, whereas with a true allegory, they would have to be.

If Lewis's purposes were not didactic or allegorical, what were they? He himself suggests three reasons for choosing the form of children's fantasy as his medium. Firstly, he felt it was the best medium to say what he wanted. He didn't write specifically *for* children at all; it was the *form* of fiction he went for. In fact, he argues that the best children's books are those which everyone can read, whatever their age – an argument that he expands in his *An Experiment in Criticism*. Secondly, if he is writing for anyone, it is himself – 'what I still like reading now that I am in my fifties'. Thirdly, there is the 'past watchful dragons' principle – a phrase taken from another essay, 'Sometimes fairy stories may say best what's to be said'. By this he means children are often on their guard against anything 'religious' since to them it means they are supposed to feel things they actually don't. Lewis believed fantasy is the best way to make children experience such things – such as the holy; or joy; or our own sinfulness; or love for Jesus.

Lewis derives fantasy from myth, and, as we have seen, he sees myth as appealing directly to our imaginations, and releasing powerful feelings which cannot necessarily be expressed intellectually. But because these can be so powerful, Christians often fear fantasy, since its misuse could be so serious. We

see this misuse today in the connection of fantasy with the occult, for example. Lewis himself clearly saw the dangers, as he saw the dangers of Romanticism. Weston's tempting arguments in *Perelandra,* where he talks of 'the force', are not far removed from some science fiction films of recent fame.

But as Lewis discovered in George Macdonald's writing, fantasy can also be used properly for good. His understanding of the psychology of C.G. Jung's archetypes helped him to see the emotional importance of fantasy; the theology of fantasy was worked out in the Inklings, and incorporated into Tolkien's 'On Fairy Stories' in *Essays Presented to Charles Williams*. As God is creator, so man is sub-creator. The worlds he creates in literature are secondary worlds, but it is still a divine activity. A true creation will parallel the unseen spiritual world that Christianity posits, and will cause our spirits to reach out in longing for its reality.

Lewis said that on first writing about Narnia, Christianity was not even intended: 'It pushed itself in of its own accord.' So we could say that while there is nothing systematic, there is an imaginative expression of Christian truths, which could bring insights to readers, whether children or not, but, in the freedom of interpretation of myth, they need not necessarily be apprehended as such. The main expressions of religious themes might be seen as:

1. Aslan's death and resurrection (though it is not a 'for everyone' substitutionary death)
2. Aslan's royalty ('the lion of the tribe of Judah')
3. the creation of the world and the entry of evil into it
4. the final judgement and the Last Day, with new heavens and a new earth
5. the nature of time (one day is as a thousand)
6. election (some animals are chosen as talking animals; the children are called into Narnia for a purpose)
7. revelation (Aslan shows himself from time to time)

We need perhaps to see, though, that certain important Christian truths are not expressed. There is little sense of in-

The High Street, Oxford, looking towards Magdalen Tower.

carnation (Aslan doesn't *become* a lion); there is little sense of the Fatherhood of God; the Holy Spirit is vague – Aslan does no more than breathe on them in *The Silver Chair* – but this is a concept notoriously difficult to get into fiction, anyway; and there is no personal devil.

These omissions should act, if nothing else does, as a warning against over-systematizing. Lewis's point is that one world is not like another; it must have enough in it of our world for us to see parallels and gain insights or take warnings, especially in terms of moral behaviour and choices; but the differences should be there, exciting our wonder and increasing our longing for 'deep heaven'.

Till we have Faces

The 1950s were prolific years for Lewis. While completing the Narnia stories, he had been fashioning his autobiography, which came out in 1955. In that year he was writing what was to be his last and favourite fiction, *Till we have Faces*, published by Geoffrey Bles the next year, and dedicated to Joy Davidman. If any of Lewis's fiction could be interpreted allegorically, this story would seem to be the one. It is based on the Greek myth of Eros (meaning love; he is the son of Venus) and Psyche (in Greek the word for soul). The story does not occur in the main body of Greek mythology, but only in a book called *The Golden Ass* by the Roman Apuleius. Psyche's beauty incurs Venus's jealousy and Eros's love; he becomes Psyche's divine lover, but she, instigated by her jealous sisters, betrays him. To win back his love Psyche has to perform three impossible tasks. She does, and is finally immortalized.

Clearly the story has possibilities as Platonic allegory, the soul's search for divine love. As such, it had haunted Lewis since he was a young man, but he could find no form in which to re-tell it: he had tried a long poem and failed. At some stage the inspiration came to tell the story through one of Psyche's sisters, whom he named Orual, using a realistic speaking-voice style. Orual's jealousy is transformed into possessive love, with all its manipulativeness and self-pity. The plot revolves round Orual's complaint against the gods for taking Psyche from her, and her enlightenment as she realizes that 'her righteousness is as filthy rags' to use a biblical phrase.

Lewis calls his story 'a myth retold', and warns against an allegorical interpretation in a letter: 'Much that you take as allegory was intended solely as realistic detail.' Allegory demands a detailed one-to-one interpretation, with flat characterization. The story Lewis tells is complex, with multi-layered interpretation, and with the fullest and most rounded characterization by far of any of his stories.

It has been suggested that Orual's character is based on Joy Davidman, who by this time was living near the Lewis brothers. But it could just as much be autobiographical, fictionally incorporating the search for faith that Lewis had been writing about a year earlier. It has also been suggested that Orual's veiling and unveiling have to do with Lewis's acknowledging part of his inner feelings suppressed for many years. Perhaps a better way to put this would be to say that in this story he most fully integrates the two sides of his character: the intellectual side, and the romantic side of myth and passion.

Certainly both sides wrestle in Orual's character. Greek myth and Christian symbol are also beautifully brought together. The title itself is an integration of Greek phrases to do with self-knowledge and ecstasy, and St. Paul's symbolism in 2 Corinthians 3:12–18, of both spiritual sight and transformation. The strength of the book lies, then, in both the complexity of its symbolic patterns and the strength of its human portrayals of beauty, self-pity and love.

The theme of human love was continued in *The Four Loves*, which was first broadcast, amid some controversy, in the U.S.A. in 1958, and then published in 1960. Between these two books came *Reflections on the Psalms*, in 1958, although Lewis had been meditating on the theme for some ten years. The influence on these two books of Joy Davidman, whom he had by now married, cannot be doubted.

Another Joy

Shadowlands

Until his mid-fifties, the shape of Lewis's life had been predictable, even given his conversion. An academic, ensconced in a safe career, with a growing reputation both as scholar and writer, he was finally rewarded in 1954 by being offered a newly-created professorial post at the university of Cambridge, the chair of medieval and renaissance literature. Mrs Moore had died, making domestic life much easier. The only problem was Warren's growing alcoholism, which was spasmodic rather than constant, but enough to cause Jack to say to Arthur: 'I embark on the "holiday" with W. full of the gloomiest forebodings. Let me have your prayers: I am tired, scared and bewildered.' For all his drinking bouts, Warren nevertheless produced a number of books, and outlived Lewis by ten years.

It was not this domestic problem that rocked Lewis's even-keeled boat. In surprising and unpredictable ways, it was a new joy that forced itself – or rather herself – into Lewis's life, even against his will, bringing him to new heights and new depths of emotion. At the time, few people knew about Lewis's marriage, and, even after Joy's death and his, close friends did not say much. It is only very recently, through the T.V. dramatization of 'Shadowlands' and Brian Sibley's book of the same name that the relationship has come to general public attention, though the facts were already known to Lewis's admirers through the biography by Roger Lancelyn Green and Walter Hooper, and Humphrey Carpenter's book on the Inklings.

As Lewis had become well-known for his Christian writings, many people wrote to him or came to him for help. As we have said, he felt it his moral duty to reply to all but the cranks. We know from the collection of letters published under the title *Letters to an American Lady* what a chore this must have been for him at times, yet each letter is courteously and helpfully written.

Magdalene College, Cambridge. Lewis was appointed Professor of Medieval and Renaissance Literature at Cambridge University in 1954.

Sheldon Vanauken's *A Severe Mercy* tells dramatically how Lewis's writings and later his friendship brought a brilliant young American couple to faith and then nurtured them in their new-found life in Christ. Poignantly, Sheldon's young wife died at much the same time as Joy did, and there was also a grieving together.

Another American who corresponded with Lewis on her way to faith was just this Joy. Born Joy Davidman, of Jewish parents from Eastern Europe who had settled in New York, she early became an atheist, then a communist. She married a fellow communist, William Gresham, and both took up writing careers. They gradually became disillusioned with communism, and William suffered a mental breakdown. In her helplessness during this time, Joy had a tremendous experience of God's presence. 'I must have been the world's most astonished atheist', she said later.

She read *The Screwtape Letters* and *The Great Divorce* and first corresponded with Lewis at that time (1950). The next year both she and her husband became Christians.

Joy talked of all her previous life as 'by comparison mere shadow play'. We are reminded of Lewis's phrase 'the shadowlands' in *The Last Battle*, where the children leave Narnia behind them at death, such was the new reality they had come into. Unfortunately, the new reality could not bind Joy and William Gresham together in what had become a problematic marriage, with two small boys, David and Douglas. Joy felt a period of separation might help, so in 1952 she came to England, inviting Lewis to join her for lunch at an Oxford hotel. He was 54, she was 37.

Two marriages
The first meeting went well, and was followed by an invitation to The Kilns for Christmas and the New Year. Joy returned to the United States in

January 1953, but it became increasingly obvious that her marriage was finished, and later that year she returned to England with the two boys, putting them to school there. Over the winter holidays all three stayed at The Kilns, and Lewis dedicated *The Horse and his Boy*, just ready for publication, to the two boys.

Lewis was in the process of vacating his rooms at Magdalen College, to take up residence at its namesake, Magdalene College, Cambridge; and Joy assisted in this. At first, Lewis wondered whether he had done the right thing in transferring to Cambridge, but he soon settled in, finding the atmosphere of a much smaller college and town congenial, his colleagues much more friendly and sympathetic, and the teaching load very much lighter. He was allowed to travel to Cambridge on Mondays and return on Fridays, and so able to continue living at The Kilns.

In 1955 Joy published an apologetic book of her own, *Smoke on the Mountain*, about the Ten Commandments – her own Jewish background being of great help. Lewis wrote the foreword to it. Even so, finances were getting tight for Joy; already Lewis had been helping with school fees, and now he suggested she move to Oxford from London, planning to help pay her rent. She took a house in Headington, and saw Lewis most days. It was quite clear to Warren by this time that she had 'designs' on Lewis – she must have fallen in love with him some time earlier. It is unclear exactly what Lewis's feelings for her were at this time. He certainly admired her for her quality of mind and quickness of wit. But he was very reluctant to talk about her, even to Arthur Greeves – he first mentions her casually only in March 1954, in connection with a testimony she had written for a collection of essays.

Then at the beginning of 1956 came the most extraordinary event, when the British Home Office refused to extend Joy's residence permit. The only way

Clare College, Cambridge from The Backs.

Lewis could see to enable her to stay was to marry her! He called it 'a pure matter of friendship and expediency', had the ceremony in a registry office, and told no-one. Clearly at this stage for him it was not a marriage at all, but a formality. Yet Lewis felt he could not keep visiting her at her house without bringing some scandal on her. Yet how could she live at The Kilns except as his real wife? So he went as far as publishing a notice of the marriage.

Then suddenly what Joy had thought of as rheumatism was diagnosed as bone cancer. She was hospitalized and bore the suffering bravely. Whether or not Lewis was in love with her before, certainly he was now. He determined on a 'proper' marriage – with a clergyman. But Joy, having been divorced, was not eligible for the rites of the Church of England. Nevertheless, God supplied an Anglican clergyman, a former student of Lewis's, from outside the diocese. The clergyman also had a gift of healing, and, at the service, offered to anoint Joy.

Slowly, healing took place. Lewis refused to hope too much. But by the end of the year, Joy was walking slowly, and after another year was able to leave hospital altogether. His own health had not been good at this time – high blood pressure and osteoporosis – and with Warren's alcoholism, there were times when Jack Lewis felt very low indeed. He tells Arthur: 'At any rate, when life gets *very* bad ... a sort of anaesthesia sets in. There is a mercy in being always tired.' Yet three months later he writes: 'Our news is all very good. Joy's improvement has gone beyond anything we dared to hope ... my osteoporosis is also very much better ... (although) I don't think I'll ever be able to take a real walk again.'

The next two years, 1958 and 1959, were happy. Warren wrote: 'What Jack's marriage meant to me was that our home was enriched and enlivened by the presence of a witty, broad-minded, well-read, tolerant Christian whom I had rarely heard equalled as a conversationalist...', though elsewhere Warren clearly misses his close one-to-one relationship with Jack.

'The Sword of Damocles', as Lewis described it, fell in October 1959; cancer spots were returning. Nevertheless the trip to Greece that Joy had set her heart on went ahead, by plane, car and wheel-chair. Lewis had not been abroad since his soldier days but went willingly, together with the Lancelyn Greens. It was wonderfully happy, according to Green's account in his biography. On their return, Joy had a mastectomy, which stayed the cancer for a short while, but it finally overtook her, and she died on 13 July 1960. Douglas Gresham wrote later: 'There were never two people alive in the history of the world who were more in love than Jack and Joy.'

A grief observed

Joy died saying to the chaplain, 'I am at peace with God.' Lewis's grief at her death was anything but peaceful. For a while he remained stunned, and then, as a way to express it, he began writing down his thoughts and feelings in four old exercise books he found in the house. When he had finished he sent them to a different publisher from his usual one, under the name of A. Clerk. They were published in 1961 under the title *A Grief Observed*. He never talked about this book, nor gave copies to any friends. Only after several years was it republished with his own name to it.

The book parallels *Till we have Faces*, in that it is a Job-like complaint against God for taking Joy from him. God remains silent, as do the gods when Orual vents her anger, rage and self-pity at them. But finally, the very silence of God became the answer, for in it is revealed deeper truths about oneself. Although much of it is self-centered, there is yet an impassioned desire to know the truth of the matter: is God really good in the way we understand good; or is there the possibility, as he first raises in *The Great Divorce*, of good not being good at all?

Lewis's grief, then, found fullest expression in a literary form – and it showed itself as a passionate doubting. The calm arguments of *The Problem of Pain* or even *The Four Loves* lie unheeded. For instance he wrote in *The Four Loves*: 'Love anything and your heart will certainly be wrung and possibly broken' and 'We shall draw nearer to God, not by trying to avoid the suffering inherent in all loves, but by accepting them and offering them to him; throwing away all defensive armour.' Such consolations seemed to be deliberately refused. Why should this have been so?

First we must realize that Lewis had been married only a few years. From what he writes here, his love was as intense as a younger man's, and a great deal more satisfying. He writes: 'What was H. [Joy] not to me? She was my daughter and my mother, my pupil and my teacher, my subject and my sovereign; and always, holding all these in solution, my trusty comrade, friend, shipmate, fellow-soldier. My mistress…' Thus the emotional intensity of first love was still with him, as well as the sense of loss of a precious gift given to him later in life when all hope of such a gift had gone.

Secondly, we need to see that Lewis was really a very black-and-white person, not just in the dialectic manner of his apologetics, but temperamentally. God is either all-loving, or all evil; his loss seems at first entirely evil. He was also a very passionate man; the academic life had disguised this as well as his boyhood fear of emotion. His biographers comment: '[the marriage was] the overwhelming fulfilment of an intense nature long unsatisfied, a tremendous capacity for love long channelled into strong friendship and immense literary creativeness.' Lastly, we may presume that grief for his mother's death, so long ago suppressed, was re-awakened; he mentions his mother's death of cancer several times in his complaint, and something of the 'grief overwhelmed in horror' about her death mentioned in his autobiography emerges now. So the terrified child grieves alongside the adult in Lewis.

Even though this may help explain the intensity of grief, we still need to ask why Lewis chose to publish such expressions. Chad Walsh, in his *The literary legacy of C.S. Lewis*, suggests that the book is something of an evil spell; but was publication needed to exorcize it? Is not such public grief merely embarrassing, and complaining against God undermining of what he had previously written?

We need here to see Lewis as a public person: it is one of the characteristics of a true artist that everything is displayed. Possibly Lewis had no thoughts of publication when he started to write, but by the third section he is clearly writing to communicate with others, not just with God or himself. We can perhaps also discern deeper purposes here: to show us that most great Christians have very real crises of faith and agony of spirit. They are not plaster saints, who make merely rhetorical gestures towards suffering. And for the sake of others who suffer such grief, they need to know this is the shape grief can take.

Did Lewis actually lose his faith? The book can be read either way, but the most natural reading is to see his faith being tested rather than destroyed. To Lewis at the time there seemed to be a destroying, but even he finally realized 'my idea of God … has to be shattered time after time'. Breakthroughs do come: he finally senses Joy's presence rather than her absence; he finally experiences bereavement as part of love. And certainly in what he wrote in the remaining few years of his own life, there is no hint of loss of faith, though 'The Seeing Eye' (1963) does dwell a great deal on façades. But his faith was not a sham, as he feared in his grief. Would Joy, whom he praised for seeing through all his sham, not have seen through that too?

King's College, Cambridge.

Teacher and Critic

The last of the dinosaurs

We now cover briefly the last few years of Lewis's life. To do this, we need to return to his move to Cambridge. Just before his appointment there he had completed his mammoth volume in the Oxford History of English Literature series (which he called 'O Hel', such a chore did it finally become). Chapter one contains a brilliant tracing of patterns of thought and literature in the sixteenth century, and then proceeds to look in more detail at certain individual writers.

Lewis did not produce any further academic writing till 1960, when his *Studies in Words* came out, followed the next year by *An Experiment in Criticism*, an interesting, if not wholly successful, attempt to set up a new approach to literary criticism and theory. Lastly, some of his Cambridge lectures were incorporated into *The Discarded Image* (1963), which could be seen as a parallel to *The Allegory of Love*, but working backwards from the Elizabethan to the medieval. After his death, Alistair Fowler put together others of his lectures in *Spenser's images of life* (1967). He also received many academic honours, in the form of honorary doctorates, though the first honour he was ever offered (a C.B.E. in 1951) he had refused.

It is the custom of newly-installed professors to give inaugural addresses. Lewis's lecture at Cambridge was given the grand title of '*De Descriptione Temporum*' (On describing the times), and the humorous alternative 'The Last of the Dinosaurs'. In it he deals mainly with matters of literary and cultural history. He concludes that since the beginning of the nineteenth century we have lived in an age different from any that has existed before – 'The Machine Age'. It is increasingly cut off from the culture of the past, including the values and beliefs of Christianity. He sees this as a decline into a new Dark Ages, and he sees himself as one of the few people still in contact with the life and traditions of our previous Western Christian culture.

This is a difficult stance to come to terms with. Certainly we are in crisis

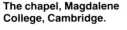

The chapel, Magdalene College, Cambridge.

times, as both *Out of the Silent Planet* and *That Hideous Strength* seek to show. But are 'we all that is left of Logres', as the latter novel expresses it? Or does Lewis rather enjoy the stance of the embattled minority, as Owen Barfield and J.A.W. Bennett suggest in *Light on C.S. Lewis*? Again, in *The Last Battle*, the feeling of the remnant is very strong. It could be argued this is entirely biblical, and we must stand, as St Athanasius once stood, unflinching in the face of heresy and the spirit of the age – an example quoted in Lewis's 'On the Reading of Old Books'. But it does tie Christianity very closely to a declining culture, and suggest an undue pessimism for the future of the faith.

Lewis was engaged at this time on one last devotional/apologetic book, completed just before his death: *Letters to Malcolm: chiefly on prayer*, begun in 1962. He had been contemplating a book on prayer for some time, but was not able to find the right form for it. Suddenly the idea of a series of imaginary letters came to him – perhaps modelled on his long correspondence with Arthur. It is no model guide on how to pray, but a probing debate into what it means to pray, to be a praying creature. The style is conversational, and it is difficult to realize that there isn't a real Malcolm at the other end, since his replies are so well imagined.

In the summer of 1961 Lewis needed an operation on his prostate gland, but because of a weakness in his heart and kidneys this was not possible. His health was very seriously undermined, partly by the hard work he had subjected himself to; partly perhaps by a diet that was, by modern standards, unwise; and partly by the growing inability to exercise in the vigorous and healthy way he had earlier. In the summer of 1963 he almost died, attended by only a few friends and Walter Hooper, a young American clergyman, whom Lewis asked to become his personal secretary. He recovered, somewhat reluctantly, but resigned his Cambridge post. Hooper returned to the United States to wind up his own affairs, and Warren returned from a holiday in Ireland. The two brothers spent two months together, waiting, as Warren

C.S. Lewis's study window can be seen in this view of Magdalene College, Cambridge.

said, 'for the new term to begin'. On 22 November 1963 Lewis slipped away quietly. He had often anticipated an entry into heaven – at the end of *The Screwtape Letters* and *The Last Battle*. Now he had come home.

Teacher and critic

Lewis's teaching career spanned forty years, representing some thirteen generations of students. Lewis's personal students included the critic Kenneth Tynan, the novelist John Wain, the writer Roger Lancelyn Green, the poet Sir John Betjeman and Professor John Lawlor. The Oxford system consists of a voluntary lecture series with compulsory weekly tutorials where each student reads out his or her assignment, which is then discussed.

Many lecturers find their lectures poorly attended, therefore. Lewis never had this problem: twice a week for six weeks, forty-five minutes each lecture, his series were popular and inspirational, as well as being scholarly and pitched at the right level. As we read them in such books as *The Discarded Image*, we sense two things: first, a clarity of mind, which is able to find significant patterns in the historic flow of literary texts; secondly, a real desire to communicate to an interested but not necessarily knowledgeable audience. Thus he is courteous, and willing to explain at some length, rather than dazzle with exhibitions of learning or technical jargon.

King's College chapel, Cambridge.

We can perhaps be a little more specific here in terms of his style. His material is very accessible: we can read an essay, say, on 'Hero and Leander', without having read the poem, and yet follow it, enjoy it and even want to read the original. He is able to convey a taste of it, quickly giving us a perception of the key concepts and its relationship with better-known works. We are treated as human beings, not as disembodied minds. Many of his examples are taken from everyday experience, and we feel our common humanity with him.

Lewis is best at commending literature; less certain in criticizing it. He tries to anticipate our difficulties in reading and divert possible prejudices. Mostly this works very well, but sometimes we are put off by having imaginary objections that we have never actually thought of loaded on to us.

As a tutor Lewis was not quite so successful. He had learned his face-to-face methods from the Great Knock – challenging statements, and 'picking an argument'. Unfortunately, most students did not enjoy such a dialectic method and were quickly reduced to confusion. He treated most of them as if they had first-class minds, already quite able to argue. It is perhaps no wonder he found tutorials rather a chore, and was relieved when, on becoming a professor, he could dispense with them.

There were perhaps other limitations. Lewis's dialectic method of arguing tends to rely on an either/or pattern of thought that sometimes reduces things too quickly to black and white. Whilst this is often a tremendous strength in philosophy or apologetics, it does not always work quite so well in dealing with literature.

A second limitation, as a teacher of English, was that most of the creative and influential thinking on the subject during the mid-twentieth century was going on at Cambridge under such people as I.A. Richards, William Empson, F.R. Leavis and E.M.W. Tillyard. Oxford had locked itself into a language versus literature struggle which ultimately proved peripheral to the mainstream of English studies.

Thus, while Lewis's academic con-

tributions to his chosen field of medieval and sixteenth-century literature were much admired, and remain required reading for students, his more general critical and theoretical thinking was not. It is not so much that it was unfashionable, but that its expression primarily in terms of Greek philosophy, either Platonic or Aristotelian, become traditional restatements of positions, ultimately adding little to a Christian philosophy of literature or engaging current thinking.

An Experiment in Criticism, written after his move to Cambridge, is his boldest effort, but it only sketches out a line of thought, and in fact raises as many questions as it answers. Lastly, being a 'lover of the past', Lewis was perhaps unduly hostile to modern literature. He shared with Barfield the belief that language was in decline; and saw the break-up of traditional literary forms as part of that decline. When we consider the achievements of a fellow convert to Christianity, T.S. Eliot, who embraced the search for new modes of literary expression, we can see just how blinkered Lewis was.

What we have positively, though, far outweighs such limitations. We have a brilliant communicator, able to awaken a love for literature in his audience. We have a scholar, with a depth of learning extending not only over his chosen field, but over several others – philosophy, classical literature, theology – with an ability to cross-reference and combine into striking generalizations – perhaps the most striking being his argument in the Oxford History that the term 'renaissance' as applied to English literary history has little, if any, meaning. His tracing of continuities represents a mind able to see original patterns amidst a mass of detailed work. As Professor Bennett said of him: 'He was a Johnsonian colossus rather than a dinosaur'.

The fighter

We have already discussed most of Lewis's major books of Christian apologetics. In one sense, of course, *all* of Lewis's work is to some extent apologetic, for it is seeking both to defend the Christian gospel and to commend it. But it is mainly from those books which come into the stricter category of apologetics that we should draw conclusions about his qualities as an apologist. There are so many points to be made generally that it is hard to know where to begin – the order chosen here has no special logic to it.

Firstly, we must note that Lewis always writes as a layman to laymen. He said once, at an 'Any Questions' session held in a factory: 'I am only a layman, and I don't know very much.' He always stated he was willing to be corrected by those who knew better, that is, professional theologians. In fact, this was a little disingenuous; he clearly knew a lot, and he clearly became increasingly distrustful of professional theologians, at the end of his life calling some of them prostitutes. But he never forgot he was talking to an 'ordinary audience'. In an interesting talk he once gave to Anglican clergy on 'Christian Apologetics', he even suggested that they should sit an exam in translating religious talk into everyday speech before being allowed into the pulpit.

For all that, his style is carefully chosen. He makes great use of analogies and images to convey his points – not just as useful examples, but because he realized that imagery speaks powerfully to the imagination, which then predisposes the intellect to hear what is being stated. His style is, as Chad Walsh states, flexible, gracious and clear. It needs to be 'modest', that is, low-key enough to allow the ideas to come through, 'transparent', yet strong enough to bear the weight of often very difficult concepts. Lewis's grounding in logical thought and good literary style come together perfectly for this task.

Lewis is a supremely confident writer: he has confidence in the rational method; in the truth of his convictions; and in the reality of his own journey to Christ, or to put it another way, of his own calling by Christ. Nevertheless, as has been pointed out, he always chose his own ground; he knew his own strengths. Yet he was not necessarily a 'safe' thinker, merely repeating in a more elegant or clever way what many had said before. He was prepared to speculate and let his imagination soar,

King's College, Cambridge.

for example in the realities of heaven and hell, into the beauty of Eden or the nature of animal pain. And it has been said rightly that Lewis, in seeking to restate traditional truths, in fact succeeds in being highly original, such is his ability to translate tradition into modern language and images.

He saw clearly that these traditional truths must be the agreed basics for all Christians. Thus he was at the same time non-denominational, convinced of the basic unity of all Christians and Christian attitudes, values and thought; yet he is also against all modern theology which waters down or demythologizes these truths. But he will not fit into an easy evangelical or liberal categorization. The most that can be said is that it is perhaps in the Church of England that such a non-partisan stance can most easily be maintained, and that if there is any 'church' colouring to his writing, it is a middle-of-the-road Anglicanism. But this has never been a barrier. His grief is at the division of Christianity, and the movement of his writing is always towards unity.

Lastly, Lewis is a fighter: sometimes his stance is that of the embattled minority; sometimes of the debater who can pick off his opponents' arguments with consummate ease. The fight is out of an uncompromising desire for truth, however unpleasant. He has no time for 'decency' or 'kindness' if they become substitutes for truth, since such decency would finally become evil. Only truth has the strength to resist evil.

A fighter needs to know both how to defend and how to attack: indeed it is often stated that the best form of defence is attack. Lewis knew this instinctively – he had a sure sense of when to

C.S. Lewis in 1955.

attack. His timing is perfect. And, to make things more difficult, he had to wage two fights at the same time. The first was against complete unbelief. His defence was that Christianity does make sense: it is not outdated, unscientific, unhistorical. His attack was that it is the *only* thing that makes sense. So he attacks the spirit of the times as 'temporal provincialism' – the contradiction of our age that says truth is all relative, and yet our relativism is absolutely right.

As early as *The Pilgrim's Regress* we get some brilliant knock-down arguments against competing philosophies – even if Christianity is difficult to make sense of, at least it is not full of the contradictions that other belief-systems contain. *The Abolition of Man* is another such frontal attack, not so much on explicit philosophies of the age, but on the unstated half-truths of the twentieth century's reductionism: everything can be explained away in terms of something else, and there is no ultimate truth of any value.

The second fight is against forms of theological unbelief. Thus Lewis's defence is that only orthodox Christianity, miracles and all, makes sense. The attack is against liberal Christianity, which he sees as likewise reductionist, busily cutting away the branch on which it is sitting in an attempt to make it palatable to modern people. He exposes its contradictions. He is not one of those 'that know [but] have grown afraid to speak', to quote *The Great Divorce*.

But he is not just a fighter; he is a superb teacher and expositor, setting out, in books like *Mere Christianity*, just what Christians believe, and how to understand Christianity's truths and mysteries correctly. He never underestimates the difficulties of believing, and in so much of his teaching we also see the imaginative artist, able to convey to us just what it feels like to be a Christian, and what certain spiritual states are like. Here we see his early search for joy fulfilled – both transcendent and yet at the same time earthly. Lewis has the artist's ability to clothe the spiritual in the physical, at the same time forming a unity, a oneness of being.

There were limitations, of course. Sometimes we feel there is an over-confidence in the rational, though some of the later books, such as *The Four Loves*, help to correct that. He himself acknowledges freely that the old-fashioned evangelist, with his straight-to-the-heart message, can often accomplish far more than his apologetic methods. This is a due humility. What is a little dangerous at times is his dialectic method of reducing options to just two: either this or that. Sometimes it works brilliantly; at other times it leads to oversimplification. Or it can lead to a rhetorical stance. We get the impression of real arguments, but when we try to use them ourselves, we never find an opponent who quite fits into the argument; or we seem to find the argument dissolves in our hands. One reason for this may be that insufficient biblical perspective is given us; Lewis does not always adequately ground us in biblical foundations.

But these are small things compared with the achievement of making Christians feel confident in their faith, and of challenging non-Christians in their disregard for Christian truth, or their complacent rejection of what is often a Sunday-school pastiche of the real thing. Lewis makes us feel the Christian gospel is powerful, to the 'breaking down of strongholds', those of the mind and those of the heart.

The critics

In trying to make a balanced assessment of Lewis's achievement, we need to face up to various criticisms that have been levelled against Lewis – at least to the sensible ones, for there are plenty of silly ones, such as that Lewis's literary criticism was sadly wanting because he did not read German! In fact, he did – but most English lecturers could be similarly indicted on such a charge.

We would expect certain groups to attack Lewis, anyway – for instance liberal theologians. After all, they are only fighting back. Or groups who have set up tests into which Lewis will not fit – such as fundamentalists. He cannot be fitted into their beliefs, say, on the inerrancy of Scripture; and, what is worse,

Father Walter Hooper, who became Lewis's secretary in his last years, and has edited many books of Lewis's essays and poems.

his life-style could be seen as very 'worldly' (even though he gave away up to two thirds of his income) since he drank and smoked. We have such criticisms at one extreme; at the other, there is uncritical veneration – whatever Lewis said must be right.

Even at the time of his writing, Lewis's attitude to women was somewhat suspect. With the growth of feminist criticism, this has been highlighted, and Lewis, for most feminists, must by now be outside the pale. In extenuation, we need to remember that he lost his mother early; had no sisters; went to all-boy schools; and attended an all-male college. Early twentieth-century academic life was very male-orientated. The woman he first came close to, Mrs Moore, he did devote himself to, even though, on his brother's account, she was demanding, silly and unable to argue logically in any way. If his female personal students found him intimidating, so did most of his male ones. When he did marry, there seems to have been a great equality between himself and Joy, as well as tremendous admiration for her. The marriage seems at the very least to disprove any charge of misogyny.

One of Lewis's earliest pre-occupations, perhaps derived from his father, and reflected even in his boyhood writ-

ing, is with cliques – a problem he found insurmountable at Malvern College. Yet in a sense the Inklings could be seen as a clique, and in *That Hideous Strength*, the clique mentality almost makes the forces of good look absurd. There is clearly a thin dividing-line between the 'remnant' idea, which is thoroughly biblical, and an 'Elijah-complex', where you need to be reminded that there are 'seven thousand who have not bowed the knee to Baal'. Perhaps again in extenuation we need to remind ourselves that for most of Lewis's life-time, the Christian church in the United Kingdom was on the decline. Yet his 'clique' mentality seems to exist apart from his faith – perhaps a little part of his personality that remained unbaptized.

Certainly, too, Lewis was a conservative by nature. Most lovers of the past are. Politically, however, he was very sceptical and uninterested – too much so for many people, who feel Lewis should have been addressing current issues more directly. Lewis was not undemocratic, however – 'free Narnia' is an important theme, as is the basic equality of its inhabitants. His views on hierarchy, which are anathema to certain egalitarians, are completely biblical, and he always defended them as such. There is, in fact, for those who

Headington Quarry Parish Church, Oxford.

look impartially, a beautiful balance between equality and hierarchy in his writings.

From a conservative theological viewpoint, certain of his views do seem questionable and unscriptural – for example, those on limbo and purgatory. It is noticeable that his views on purgatory get in the way of his finding consolation in *A Grief Observed* – Joy will merely continue her suffering there. And, as Michael Christensen points out in his *C.S. Lewis on Scripture*, Lewis's views on the Bible would probably please neither liberal nor fundamentalist. These views are not obtrusive, however, since his main job was to concentrate on the basic truths of the faith, which are entirely orthodox.

In these days of what might be termed the 'occult explosion', Lewis's references to magic and even astrology become problematic – even though harmless when first written. The tendency of fantasy writing for children has today unfortunately veered towards the occult. Lewis cannot be blamed for that, but the attempt to explain Christian mysteries in terms of 'deep magic' has to be rejected, since the connotations are now all wrong.

None of these criticisms can really be

considered damning when weighed against the very obvious merits of his life and work. In fact, it could be argued that the most serious limitations are actually none of the above, but those mentioned in the last section: an over-confidence, at times, in human reason, and an oversimplification into an either/or dialectic which does not quite reach people where they are. But in everything he did, there was a massive honesty, an integrity, and a grasp of truth which brings great solidity. With someone like this, critical arrows often bounce back on to the archer.

Lewis's achievement

How does one measure a person's achievement, especially when he has such a multi-faceted life as Lewis? We could start with the measurable – for instance, sales of his books. Current figures suggest that the annual sale of the fifty or so books Lewis wrote now approaches two million, about half of which is accounted for by the seven Narnia chronicles. Certainly these figures show no sign of abating. Usually, after twenty-five years, most authors' popularity begins to wane – not so Lewis's. In fact, between his death and 1975, sales of his books trebled!

Individual titles have equally impressive records: *The Screwtape Letters* was reprinted eight times before the end of 1942; total sales of its paperback editions now touch one million. C.S. Lewis societies have sprung up, especially in the United States where his popularity is somewhat greater than in the United Kingdom.

We might prefer to judge Lewis's achievement in terms of human lives changed. We have many such testimonies. Sheldon Vanauken we have already mentioned. He comments on Lewis's gift of friendship, 'withal, the most genial of companions.' Vanauken both read, wrote to and met Lewis.

But many have been changed just by reading his books. One of the most remarkable testimonies of this in recent years is that of Charles Colson, imprisoned for his part in the Watergate affair of ex-President Nixon. While in prison he read *Mere Christianity*, and was struck by the intellectual and logical quality of its defence of Christianity, and by its exposure of human pride. He felt the book spoke exactly to his condition, and testifies to its being an important step in his conversion. As a result of this he founded the Prisoners' Christian Fellowship.

So far, we have measured achievement by what Lewis wrote and did. But very often literary figures such as Dr Johnson have become famous, not just by what they did, but also who they were as people. Lewis certainly seemed to have a similar charismatic quality, indelibly impressing people who met him. A former student, Kenneth Tynan, remembered him for his prodigious memory, his debating skill, his ability to make his chosen field of literary study come alive, and his pastoral concern and humanity.

Jocelyn Gibb collected the comments of close friends in *Light on C.S. Lewis* just after Lewis's death. His friend Nevill Coghill's remarks are particularly apt. He, too, makes the parallel with Johnson. On the other hand, Lewis's stepson David Gresham wrote in a letter that he remembers Lewis being clumsy, irascible and nervous.

Perhaps the most amusing anecdote is that of Lewis's taxi-driver, Clifford Morris. Sometimes he would drive Lewis to Cambridge instead of his taking the train. They might stop at transport cafés for Lewis's compulsory cup of tea. Morris remembers Lewis 'sitting in the middle of a crowd of lorry drivers ... while he enthralled them with his wit and conversational powers.' This shows something of the humility of Lewis and his enjoyment of the society of his fellow human-beings, his ability to stay in touch with them despite the ivory towers of Oxbridge.

We can perhaps best sum up his achievement by saying that here is a man who has really made an impact on his world. And his world is not just the academic one; it is that of the university of life as experienced by mid-twentieth century men, women and children. It is, if you like, the 'post-Christian' world of modern western civilization. His achievement here was to bring old truth and give it new relevancy and vitality in a secular age, and to challenge the new complacencies of that age. Part of his continuing impact must be that those complacencies are now well and truly shaken, and people are now more open to reconsider beliefs that claim ultimacy and truth.

Lewis must also be seen as one of those people used by God to turn around the spiritual current or flow of an age. Orthodox Christianity was on the retreat at the time of his conversion – undermined by both liberal theology and scientific and secular scepticism. At his death, the Christian church in the United Kingdom, and even more so in the United States, was entering renewal, with Christians emerging from their ghetto with new confidence and hope. Lewis's impact must be acknowledged in this.

Whilst Lewis was very traditional in his attitude to worship and church structures, he was radical in the completeness of his conversion – it entered practically every part of his life, so that we feel he really engaged with the world as it actually existed. Even his last essay 'We have no "Right to Happiness"', shows him addressing contemporary problems, not in despairing gestures, but as a logical, reasonable defender of traditional Christian morality, his thought built on a massive foundation of truth, honesty and experience. It is his massive balance that stays with us, the balance of imaginative faith and radiant hope, in the spirit of love and charity.

C.S. Lewis's gravestone at Headington Quarry.

Books mentioned

with original publishers and dates and first paperback editions.

The Pilgrim's Regress: An allegorical apology for Christianity, reason and romanticism (Dent, 1933; Eerdmans, 1958; Collins Fount)
The Allegory of Love: A study in medieval tradition (Clarendon Press, 1936)
Out of the Silent Planet (John Lane, 1938; Pan, 1952)
Perelandra (John Lane, 1943) = *Voyage to Venus* (Pan, 1960)
That Hideous Strength: a modern fairy-tale for grown-ups (John Lane, 1945; abridged for Pan, 1955)
The Personal Heresy: a Controversy, with E.M.W. Tillyard (Oxford U.P., 1939)
The Problem of Pain (Centenary Press, 1940; Collins Fontana, 1957)
The Screwtape Letters (Geoffrey Bles, 1942; Collins Fontana, 1955)
A Preface to Paradise Lost (Oxford U.P., 1942)
The Abolition of Man (Oxford U.P., 1943; Collins Fount, 1978)
The Great Divorce: a dream (Geoffrey Bles, 1945; Collins Fontana, 1972)
Miracles: a preliminary study (Geoffrey Bles, 1947; Collins Fontana, 1960)
Mere Christianity (a revised edition of *Broadcast Talks, Christian Behaviour* and *Beyond Personality*) (Geoffrey Bles, 1952; Collins Fontana, 1955)
The Dark Tower and other stories ed. Walter Hooper (Collins, 1977)

The Narnia Chronicles
The Lion, the Witch and the Wardrobe (Geoffrey Bles, 1950; Penguin/Puffin, 1959)
Prince Caspian (Geoffrey Bles, 1951; Penguin/Puffin 1962)
The Voyage of the Dawn Treader (Geoffrey Bles, 1952; Penguin/Puffin, 1965)
The Silver Chair (Geoffrey Bles, 1953; Penguin/Puffin, 1965)
The Horse and his Boy (Geoffrey Bles, 1954; Penguin/Puffin, 1965)
The Magician's Nephew (Bodley Head, 1955; Penguin/Puffin, 1963)
The Last Battle (Bodley Head, 1956; Penguin/Puffin, 1964)

English Literature in the Sixteenth Century (O.H.E.L. Vol. 3) (Clarendon Press, 1954)
Surprised by Joy: The shape of my early life (Geoffrey Bles, 1955; Collins Fontana, 1959)

Till we have Faces: a myth retold (Geoffrey Bles, 1956; Collins Fount, 1978)
Reflections on the Psalms (Geoffrey Bles, 1958; Collins Fontana, 1961)
The Four Loves (Geoffrey Bles, 1960; Collins Fontana, 1963)
A Grief observed (Faber and Faber, 1961)
An Experiment in Criticism (Cambridge U.P., 1961)
The Discarded Image: An introduction to medieval and renaissance literature (Cambridge U.P., 1964)
Letters to Malcolm: chiefly on prayer (Geoffrey Bles, 1964; Collins Fontana, 1966)
Spenser's images of life ed. Alastair Fowler (Cambridge U.P., 1967)
Selected literary essays ed. Walter Hooper (Cambridge U.P., 1969)

Letters
Letters of C.S. Lewis ed. W.H. Lewis (Geoffrey Bles, 1966)
Letters to an American Lady ed. Clyde Kilby (Eerdmans, 1967)
Mark vs. Tristram: Correspondence between C.S. Lewis and Owen Barfield ed. Walter Hooper (1967)
They Stand Together: Letters to Arthur Greeves ed. Walter Hooper (Collins, 1979)

Collections of essays, talks, sermons
Essays Presented to Charles Williams with others (Oxford U.P., 1947)
They asked for a Paper (Geoffrey Bles, 1962)
Screwtape proposes a toast (Collins Fontana, 1965)
Christian reflections ed. Walter Hooper (Geoffrey Bles, 1967)
Undeceptions: Essays on theology and ethics ed. Walter Hooper (Geoffrey Bles, 1971), redistributed into –
  God in the Dock (Collins Fount, 1979) and
  First and Second Things (Collins Fount, 1985) and (in the U.S.A.)
  The Grand Miracle (Eerdmans, 1970; Ballantine, 1983)
Of this and other Worlds ed. Walter Hooper (Collins Fount, 1982)

Books about C.S.Lewis
Humphrey Carpenter: *The Inklings* (Allen & Unwin, 1978)
Michael Christensen: *C.S. Lewis on scripture* (Hodder, 1980/Word, 1979)
Jocelyn Gibb ed.: *Light on C.S. Lewis* (Geoffrey Bles, 1965)
R.L. Green and Walter Hooper: *C.S. Lewis: a biography* (Collins, 1974)
Walter Hooper: *Past Watchful Dragons* (Macmillan N.Y., 1979/Collins, 1980)

John Peters: *C.S. Lewis: the Man and his Achievement* (Paternoster, 1985)
Brian Sibley: *Shadowlands* (Hodder & Stoughton, 1985)
Chad Walsh: *The literary legacy of C.S. Lewis* (Sheldon Press, 1979)

Other books
Sheldon Vanauken: *A Severe Mercy* (Hodder & Stoughton, 1977)
Charles Colson: *Born Again* (Hodder & Stoughton, 1979)